COLLECTED POEMS

W. R. RODGERS

COLLECTED POEMS

*With an Introductory Memoir
by Dan Davin*

London
OXFORD UNIVERSITY PRESS
NEW YORK   TORONTO
1971

Oxford University Press, Ely House, London W1

GLASGOW NEW YORK TORONTO MELBOURNE WELLINGTON
CAPE TOWN SALISBURY IBADAN NAIROBI DAR ES SALAAM LUSAKA ADDIS ABABA
BOMBAY CALCUTTA MADRAS KARACHI LAHORE DACCA
KUALA LUMPUR SINGAPORE HONG KONG TOKYO

ISBN 0 19 211809 9

Printed in Great Britain
by The Bowering Press Plymouth

CONTENTS

ACKNOWLEDGEMENTS

Acknowledgements are due to Martin Secker & Warburg Ltd., who first published *Awake! and Other Poems* in 1941 and *Europa and the Bull and Other Poems* in 1952; also to the Editor of the *Irish Times*, in which 'Home Thoughts from Abroad' first appeared; to Grabhorn-Hoyem, California, who printed 'Field Day' as a broadsheet; and to Benham and Company, who first printed 'Requiem for Michael' in *Essex Roundabout* in 1963.

W. R. Rodgers's uncollected poems, with the exception of 'Field Day' and 'Lament for an Educated Hole in the Road', were read on the B.B.C. Third Programme.

INTRODUCTORY MEMOIR

A while ago in Dublin I found myself bailed up in the Bailey and agreeing to subscribe to a fund for restoring a Presbyterian church, and in Ulster at that. Me, brought up a Catholic by Irish parents from Galway and Cork—people for whom the North meant, not our New Zealand North (a hot, soft place), but the Black North Ulster, full of Black Protestants and bigoted Orangemen. It was the oldest Presbyterian church in Ireland, this one, at Loughgall in Armagh. But what if it was? What was that to me, a defaulter from a church far older? The people who had prayed first at Loughgall were my ancestors, Catholic. The people praying there now, if Protestants could pray, were planted supplanters.

Was too much Guinness the explanation, then, or the sheer paradox of the thing? Or the great brown eyes, those of her father dead not long since, that Harden Rodgers turned on me? Something of that, yes; but more the story, told with her and his wry smile, of how the pulpit in Loughgall was so high that, on those Sundays when Saturday had been the night before, Bertie—as even that staid parish knew its pastor—could stoop in a pause of his preaching, some cautiously contrived colon, and retch gently, invisible to his devout and Sunday-sombre flock.

I tried then to remember whether I had met him or his legend first. In my memory it seemed to be the legend. Ulstermen who had known him in those years of his ministry—1934 to 1946— recalled life then in Bertie's house as a sort of poem, one of his own poems. There was always sun or moonlight on apple-blossom, endless talk of life and death in the small big house full of books and the small hours that never grew smaller, and a gay drift of laughing girls flitting innocently carnal through the orchard. And somewhere at the heart of it all would be Bertie, smoking his eschatological pipe, nodding a compassionate head to the saint and sinner in others and himself, anticipating indiscretion, confession, disclosure, revelation, with the omniscience of his calm 'I know, I know".

He was a great reader of the earlier English poets in those days, trying to sidestep the rancorous antimonies of Ulster, and perhaps he was hoping to re-create a parochial idyll and idol of Herrick. At the least he would have been young enough and sanguine to think with the roadmender who once answered an inquiry after his health: 'God is good; and the devil isn't bad, thank God'.

This picture that his old friends called up was certainly not the Black North, or the Presbyterian Minister, that I had been prepared for. And it may be that the grimmer vision was the more typical than Bertie's legend, though I can doubt this as I don't doubt those girls, the talk, the laughter, and the apple-blossom. For these fit more easily with the man I later came to know.

It was some time in 1948 that we first met. Two years had passed since my transition from the New Zealand Division to the Clarendon Press—hardly more than a change of unit, it sometimes seemed—and I had published a book or two of my own. Bertie's *Awake! and Other Poems* had been published in 1941 when I was elsewhere but people still remembered it and thought well of it. Louis MacNeice, I gathered, had brought him over to London at the end of the war and Laurence Gilliam had given him a job in Features at the B.B.C. His wife Marie, a psychiatrist, was working in a clinic in Edinburgh and Bertie was living with friends in Wapping. I assumed he was whatever might be the Presbyterian equivalent of a 'spoiled priest'.

We would have met in a pub somewhere, through friends. Not Soho, probably—the tide of literary life had already ebbed from there. It might have been the Lamb in Lamb's Conduit Street. Bloomsbury had only just begun to succumb to the arrogance of modern architects and the fungoid university. There was still a neighbourhood in Mecklenburgh Square and the streets round about. More probably, though, we met in the Stag's Head near the B.B.C. where lunchtimes lasted through opening hours and where it was hard to distinguish poets from producers, since the roles were often doubled and neither would have been altogether embarrassed at being taken for the other, in those days before the Fall, before radio was consigned to the Age of Steam and the world became a global suburb.

Meeting him for the first time, I remember sensing in him the decent pride and reserve of 'your quiet man' but it was not a glacis that a stranger had to cross, as it was with Louis. The brown eyes were large, luminous, slightly nocturnal. There were laughter wrinkles about them, though down-turning like the corners of the mouth, and so suggesting irony and wryness, the afterthoughts felt simultaneously with the gaiety they would succeed to, the bone of bitterness that is beneath and supports the ripple of Irish laughter. His voice was low and pleasant and the nuances intertwined in it like the colours in the Irish tweed he usually wore. There was a calm in him, like that of someone who was as much a witness as a doer. His dignity was that of a man who respected all men, and himself among them, not like the irritable dignity of teachers, or N.C.O.'s, or spinsters in public life—people who fear that their authority is greater than their presence and must be continually reasserted. So, though you felt in him a passionate man, he moved calmly through other people's contentions and animosities and neither attracted nor emanated truculence.

Not long after we met I conceived a plan for a book—one still to be published—which was to be called 'The Character of Ireland'. The editors I wanted were Bertie himself, and Louis MacNeice. This project was to become, as things turned out, the thread—I can hardly say rosary and worry-beads would imply comfort—that would twine through what was left of their lives and perhaps what is left of mine.

In the summer of 1949 I went to Belfast and Dublin, my first visit since the war. Bertie had armed me with introductions and I saw Belfast through his eyes and those of his friends—Sam Hanna Bell, John Hewitt, George McCann, James Boyce, John Stewart, and others. It was a more humane and friendly city than I would otherwise have seen, mediated through these men in Kelly's Wine Vaults, and many another pub with snug cubicles still haunted by Wolfe Tone. And in Dublin, too, I met his skein of friends, in the Pearl Bar where Smyllie of the *Irish Times* presided and in the Gresham Hotel where Peadar O'Donnell drank coffee and gave whisky to his friends. This too, the Dublin of Austin Clarke, Donagh McDonagh, Paddy Kavanagh, Theo Moody, Ben Kiely,was a Dublin—or Dublins —it would have taken me a long time to find without Bertie's help, a place where every man had a self of his own which at one time or another he had permitted Bertie to see. For if in a sense he had created the Belfast he showed me, he had himself in a sense been recreated by Dublin.

Domiciled in London now, he was, like a true expatriate, intensely preoccupied with the country—the two countries—he had left. These were the years when he was doing his best work for the B.B.C., the series of mosaic portraits made after the formula he had himself originated, of Irish writers—A.E., Yeats, Joyce, the great men of Ireland in our time. It was natural, then, that the book I suggested should attract him. Plans went forward rapidly at first, reticulating and ramifying like a page from the Book of Kells. Conferences with him and Louis were frequent and agreeable, though seldom exactly according to arrangements. I recall a day in June 1949 when I cleared my desk of all appointments so as to devote all my time to my two editors. I had yet to learn that for Bertie 'Journeys are always curly'. The afternoon passed and they didn't come. It was after nine that evening when the telephone at home hooked me from the deep water of my study, where I was working on a book about the battle of Crete. Bertie's voice, full of whisky and placation, reported himself and Louis and Dylan Thomas bogged down at the George in Oxford. Would I join them?

No more work was done that night. The George foreclosing, the conference that was not a conference adjourned to my house. It was early morning when I retired to bed and my two editors set off in high spirits to look at Oxford empty in the summer dawn and to visit Ernest Stahl who had been helping Louis with a broadcast version of Goethe's *Faust*. Dylan had capitulated an hour or two earlier and been put to bed in our attic. He awoke to learn over a lunchtime pint that they had been stopped by police who wanted to know what Louis had in his rucksack. 'But didn't you tell him, Louis, that you never travelled with anything but a change of verse and a clean pair of rhymes?'

The plan formed, the authors chosen and persuaded to promise performance, we settled down to wait for the articles. Louis went off to Athens as Director of the British Institute, and nothing much happened until he came back at the beginning of 1952. There was some question of whether they had been paid the expenses of the visit to Oxford three years before. In reply to my apology, Bertie wrote: 'You say "You will remember we discussed"—I don't remember. Not "in vino veritas", but "in risu veritas". I remembered only that I wished to see you, was intent on seeing you, and did see you. The other kind of money, with us Irish people, is something to forget with. And may I be allowed to forget what I said? And will you be forgetful enough to allow? I should be grateful. I look forward to seeing you in Oxford.'

This airy dismissal of money was an agreeable and polite flourish only, not meant to take me in or himself either. We knew well enough even then, when he was regularly employed, that he was never likely to have, would not expect or want to have, 'the other kind of money' or any kind of money in the quantities you needed if you were ever to forget about it for long. Indeed, by the end of the following year, the hard fact could not be escaped. His first wife was dead. He had got married again, to Marianne, the former wife of Laurence Gilliam. She was to prove a meet helpmeet through his remaining life, and there were some difficult days ahead. He had become a free lance—was there ever a lance that was free, except in the sense of unemployed?—and he was at the end of his tether. He had to take a job with an advertising agency. The only slogan of his that I can recall was invented for some detergent or domestic cleanser: 'Is your Father a Mother or your Mother a Feather?'. I do not think it was considered suitable, or that his services were long retained.

Meanwhile, 'The Character of Ireland' was not coming forward as well as it might. The reliable had sent in their articles, the others not. Threats and cajolery issued from the two editors. From time to time one or other of them would track down the recalcitrant in London, Belfast or Dublin. But the subsequent discussion would normally take place in a pub, reproach would dissolve in jest or be so muffled and roundabout that it wasn't even perceived, and if the talk adverted again to its original purpose the reproach would be tainted and weakened by a fear of discourtesy. Promises would be made by the laggard, as a concession to his host's discomfort and not as of right. And, as Dr. Johnson remarks, authors' promises are as readily forgotten as lovers' vows.

Nor were the editors able to cite example from themselves. The plan at this stage was that they should each write a poem for the book. In September, Bertie had written and explained: 'In a moment of insight (or drink) I therefore suggested that Louis and I should devote the middle and hinging pages of the book to a pastoral hammer-and-tongs give-and-take on Partition, in which we might, as uncouth shepherds, say all the outrageous things which nobody dare put in urbane prose: Ireland forgives anything in poetry. Louis, I'm glad, likes the idea.'

For them as procrastinating poets the idea had an obvious advantage: they need not write until all the other articles were in. As editors it gave them the consolation that the delays of others meant all the more time for them to meditate. So they shuttled and shuffled, sometimes alternately and sometimes together, between England and Ireland, sometimes on business for the B.B.C., sometimes for family reasons, and sometimes for our book; but basically because, though England kept them, Ireland drew them. The one country gave them a living; the other, life.

Once they returned with a tale of a railway crossing they had come to and found half-closed, somewhere in the West of Ireland. They eventually found the crossing-keeper in a pub not far away. 'But why did you leave the gate half-open?' Louis asked. 'Well, you see, sir, I was half-expecting a train.'

There were times when I felt that they themselves were only half-expecting and I myself began to stop expecting at all. Year followed year and I tried every exhortation. Sometimes cash seemed the most likely stimulus. As one contributor put it: 'We Irish are, as you know, a deeply spiritual people, and the slower we are paid the more spiritual we get.' And Jim Phelan, by that standard the least spiritual since the fastest and most exigent of our contributors, followed up his article on tinkers by driving his gypsy caravan to Oxford and appearing in our office to collect his fee.

But there was always some new delay, vexatious and redoubtable. Someone's pseudonym was leaked and he had to withdraw his indiscretion, leaving us to find another writer. Another was in the Government and decided he couldn't risk saying what he now thought ought to be said. Dylan Thomas died and Louis, as a literary executor, was deep in new responsibilities. Some contributors ratted, repented, and ratted again. When my letters became fierce instead of plaintive, one or other of the editors would arrive in Oxford to placate or reassure or to tie me up in a night-long cocoon of good but bemusing talk, that made reproach impossible. They usually took away and left behind a hangover, sometimes something else. Hence a worried note from Bertie in 1955: 'Have you seen in your office or at home, a little rounded metal tobacco-box, part of my pocket penates, which I sadly miss?'

In June the next year Bertie came down for Auden's Inaugural Lecture as Professor of Poetry. He was tenacious in the ceremonial of friendship. David Cecil gave a party afterwards. Over in a corner of the room, where the drinks were, I can still see them, each filling his glass in turn, and the heads going up as the drinks go down, tongues in full spate and laughter. After such an evening as this, we would usually go back to my house, where Bertie would be staying. As the whisky grew lower in the bottle, his voice would grow lower also. Craning to hear what he was saying, I would marvel half-resentfully at the skill of his monologue. To have any hope of getting an aria of your own, you would have to listen intently to try and find a gap where you might break in. So he started with the advantage of your attention. But there wouldn't be a gap. He used Scheherezade's technique of the unended anecdote, like unclosed parentheses, so that you could never cut him off.

Anecdote was the staple of his conversation at such times. He mistrusted the abstractness of pure argument, its tendency to polarize; he did not like talk to have a border, its North and South. The advantage of a story was that the individual had flesh on it, was unique; and, since somewhere in his recesses there still seethed a preacher, the anecdote for him still carried elements of the parable.

Thus he would tell a cherished tale of a parishioner rebuked for some transgression who had replied: 'Never mind, your reverence, the devil'll never light a whin-bush at your backside for my mistakes.' And he would smile and pull on his pipe and leave you to draw the moral and to infer also, if you liked, that the parishioner knew, or Bertie thought he knew, that the shepherd was one of his own black sheep. Black sheep or not, it was clear that his affection for the people of his parish was partly a reflection of their fondness for him.

Or, to illustrate the love-hate between North and South he

would recall the man challenged at the Border. 'Friend or foe?'
No reply and your man comes on, boots loud in the dark.
'Friend or foe? Answer or I fire.' 'Foe.' 'Pass, foe.'
But in the end the soliloquy of that blackthorn mind would
pass to reverie. His low, withdrawn mumble would be less and
less audible, or comprehensible. But if his host, thinking of bed,
pressed him too hard for his meaning, the sharp reprimand
could still flash from the crepuscular, 'If you were as drunk as I
am you'd know what I was talking about'. For, behind the
obscure double turnings of his talk as such times, there was
still a thread of theme, and he was still pursuing, and being
pursued:

> A tether that held me to the hare
> Here, there, and everywhere.

We were in 1956 now, and on the last day of August, Bertie
reported: 'I have started my Epilogue, meaning it to be a kind
of requiem or "wake" for the dead of Ireland; and what else
was Ireland ever, but her dead?' This was to encourage me to
produce some expenses for his visit to Ireland, planned for
September, 'first making sure that the foxes are at home'.

After he came back he was much preoccupied with the tapes
that he had accumulated, then and over the years, of his talks
with the great Irish survivors. If I would co-operate, with
money, and let him have a session with Peadar O'Donnell, 'I'd
get you the best stuff that ever was got under the Irish lamps.'
And there was Richard Best he had recorded and many another.

But there was still no finished book and in March 1957 I
evidently had to be reassured once more and thanked for I have
forgotten what favour.

And may I say, after all my undeserving, that the world
whittles itself down finely to a few persons who matter to me,
and you are one of the Gideon's army. Or, may I put it
another way, and extend—though not extenuate—the state-
ment and say primitively that you bring me luck? I arrive
here to find that the waiting letters largely resolve my im-
mediate problem. I'm a problem, of course, that will find its
answer on its death-bed (I'm thinking of patenting an elastic
bed in order to prolong life). Notice my commas and full-
stops; they are very careful ones: they have to be. 'Young

man,' said A.E. to Joyce who undergraduately brought his poems, written on purple paper—purple birds of passage—for A.E. to give an opinion on, 'Young man, you have not enough chaos in you to be a poet.' Only an Ulsterman, like A.E., would ever know the importance of having a pre-destined chaos. 'We don't want order,' said Harry Brogan (the Abbey actor, the only one) to me . . . 'We don't want order. And we don't want disorder. What we want is orderly disorder. I don't know,' says he (describing a figure of eight on the table with his wet pint of stout), 'how it adds up. But it does.'

Let's now get down to business. (Oh, before I leave it, a story about Brogan. Kavanagh said to me lately that lately Brogan said to him in a moment of midnight confidence—'Seumas, my mother was a corpse-washer in Dublin, and once she took me with her to help turn over a big woman of twenty-two stone. I was a very impressionable age, Seumas, I was only eight at the time, and things like that could turn you against things. But thanks to God, Seumas, I'm married and have a very nice family.')

You and me have a lot to be thankful for. But now to business . . .

One last thing:— I read to you last night, Richard Best talking about Bergin. Sarah Purser painted Bergin's portrait and asked me round to see it. I remember Douglas Hyde was there, and Hyde, when the portrait was hoisted on the easel, said, 'Who is it? Who is it?' And she looked very crestfallen. 'Is it a judge?' 'Yes,' I said, 'it's the judge of us all. It's Bergin.'

And now—I shall write, myself—would you, on the heels of last night, say a good word for me to the Judge of Us All?

Five years passed. Most of the articles had come in, some of them had gone out again, and some had come back, revised. Others, meanwhile, needed to go out again, having gone out of date. But we seemed in sight of the end, except for Louis' pro-logue and Bertie's epilogue. Louis was at length persuaded to commit himself to a date. He did not like committing, especially himself, because he kept his word more than most. He did so now and in 1958 it was delivered. Bertie's poem was promised for the

Christmas of 1960. Christmas came but not the epilogue. Contributors grew restless again, clamouring to be paid or published. Some had already gone home and taken their immortal wages.

I really wanted that poem of Bertie's but by the end of 1962 I was threatening to do what a more sensible man would have done long before; to call the whole thing off. Bertie's reply, tactfully deferred to the day after April Fools' Day, 1963, pleased and perhaps fooled me. He was writing in bed 'wrapped in a fur of wheezes'. But 'I'm working away at the Epilogue and am doing nothing else. Only I'd be grateful if you would give me another week or so, for it's all in bricks at the moment which have to be architected.' There had been desperate crises with a landlord and it was doubtful how long they could stay at Rookery Farm near Colchester.

I gave him seven weeks. Or, rather, seven weeks passed before I could bring myself to turn from many other pressing things and decide we were no further ahead. I showed both editors a draft letter which I proposed to send to surviving contributors. It was to explain why the project must now be considered to have predeceased them. Louis' answer proposed a conference and magnanimously avoided blame to Bertie. Bertie's reply was written the day after he got my letter and while it was still stinging:

> indeed I *have* been working at the Epilogue. . . . But I have been frustrated, distracted, tormented and halted by trouble with landlord and solicitors—and the domestic reverberations of it. . . . I'll send you, this weekend, bits of what I've already written, and I'll drive urgently ahead with the whole thing. And I'd be truly grateful if you would hold your hand for the next week or two till I finish it.

Before the week he sued for was over he sent me, on 28 May, his finished lines with prose intercalations about how the gaps were to be filled, a sort of preview and 'earnest' of the epilogue, and necessarily a brief one.

> Working on it both excites and depresses me, and I realize that to write about it is like opening an old wound, which is Ireland. However, it is no doubt good for me to do it, and to get rid—in a governed way—of deeply ungoverned bitterness and admiration. I sit here with a little hill before me, of notes,

comments, reminiscences, confessions, phrases, lines of verse, thoughts unthought of, all gathered over mountainous years of trouble and love, and I wonder which way the water—the poetry—which shows the shape of the land, is going to run down it. Will it run, and will the stones obligingly melt? And what dark cloud might pour, on second thought? I have too much, in the past, waited for poetry to run, as one waits for a gift, but gifts get fewer as one waits knowingly for them to come. As Dylan said to me once, 'a man's will must be stronger than his gifts'. One must prime the pump. I have 'will' and wilfulness enough, God knows, to rebuild the hill (apart from depressions) but will it flow? Anyhow, here is the first run ('the first run', they say of Irish whiskey, is fatal; it has to be distilled again and again) for what it's worth. I have to go to Dublin at the end of June, for a Fred Higgins programme, and this epilogue—or I—must be finished before that, and in your hands. It'll take me all my time, resenting myself as I do. But I wish I could get the first wilful run of it, and then find the easy will-less expansion of it.

To me this first run, these fragments shored up against what I still hoped would not be a ruin, were fine and promised a great poem; and also to the colleagues to whom, lest I be besotted, I showed it for confirmation and reassurance. There was nothing for it but to applaud, and to turn to other work in order to forget one's impatience.

But fifteen years had passed and we were now in that time when we must take life not as it comes but as it goes. On the morning of 30 August that year a friend and I tracked Louis down to St. Leonard's hospital where he had been brought in sudden illness, Louis whom we had all taken for granted as an iron man. An oxygen cylinder leaned its menacing aid against the wall. His face was pewter. His eyes, lack-lustre, smiled for us but looked far beyond us. His voice was weak, his breath short. To try and cheer him, I told him of a plan to re-issue a book of his. The faint smile was courtesy to my intention, rather than a poet's pleasure. We withdrew after a few minutes, shattered. I had seen men, their bullets fatal, with that colouring, that look. He died early on 3 September.

At the funeral service in St. John's Wood Church, Louis'

world of friends, a bigger world and more various than any of us would have guessed, came together, some of them apart. In the pub afterwards, Louis unheard now and unseen still with us, we held a hurried wake. Bertie told me that from this time forward the Epilogue, an epilogue to Louis, must be prior to everything, the finished book would be memorial.

In October I was myself in Dublin, where Louis was still mourned. It might be true, the saying Bertie had once repeated to me, a saying of Cruise O'Brien's father, that Dublin was a holy city where 'a citizen might see a sparrow fall to the ground every day and God watching it'.

If God was not watching Bertie's own landfall there in July 1964, Bertie was no doubt keeping a corner of his eye on God; perhaps even deputizing a little, to judge by the Old Testament echo of what he wrote to me from there:

> Probably my reason in going was to vivify my anger and love for the place and to find out why it was always so destructive to the likes of Louis and me. I think that I have found out part of the reason, and I want in some way to get it into the *Epilogue* of the book. If you can bear with me just a bit longer—I think you said September some time ago—I'll send you a screed. It wasn't an easy visit. I had an *A.E.* programme and a *1916 Easter Rising* one to deal with, and every day for five weeks I'd to turn myself into a successful extrovert. I think I managed to do it, more equably than usual. But in the small hours of each morning my introverted mind, outraged, had to go mad. A.E.—Yeats—Dev—Cosgrave etc., all the old timers—and all the Words I'd heard about them, would go berserk, become alive, and rampage through my brain with a will of their own but I managed to keep a hold, and to return to civilization.

That November Laurence Gilliam died, closing for ever his own old wound, opening for others a new one of loss and grief. My own work meanwhile at the office had become ever more demanding, it was more than ever difficult to salvage the energy to write my own stuff, and the thought of Bertie and his epilogue recurred to me only when I was too tired to prevent it and too pessimistic to pursue it. If I was blocked by lack of time to write, Bertie, it now seemed to me, was a hopeless case of writer's block from less external causes. To write the Epilogue he needed to be, not merely the poet he was, but his own confessor, his own priest, his own psycho-analyst. I now doubt whether he was any longer able to make the necessarily appalling self-confrontation. But, then, I rather agreed with him that material uncertainty, the quotidian anxieties of forever having to find money by ephemeral preoccupations which could not guarantee tomorrow, were the cause. I listened with sympathy to his despair of the hand-to-microphone life, and hoped that he might somehow escape, if only by his own formula, 'Necessity is the mother of circumvention'.

So, like so many of his ancestors and mine, he decided he would cross the Atlantic, go West. I tried to help him to some poetic residency on an American campus. And in February 1966 he wrote to thank me.

I have not ignored or neglected the 'Epilogue'. I'm writing some good stuff for it, only it takes a lot of architecting. Also I have to go off on tangents, like organizing Arts Council grants and jobs for young writers in N. Ireland; lecturing, to keep the wolf from the door ('in case', as Myles naGopaleen puts it, 'he should get out'); finishing a most crying out B.B.C. script for *The Easter Rising*. I'm also, despite it all, keeping at the Epilogue, and I think I'm getting my voice back. An incidental, but exacting, bother is that once I get into the Epilogue it starts other hares in my mind and I tend to fly off in pursuit of them and have to remind myself that I haven't the time and that they'll run another day. Like this poem to childhood (I must have started a dozen or two scattered stanzas of it) of which these random stanzas are a sample:

> When I was young
> The day was forever and ever,
> And the bed said
> 'Amen'.

> The doorknob then
> Was big and sticky with jam, and my
> Forefinger said
> 'I am'....

... It could go on forever in a half-autobiographical way, half melancholy, half gay, but mounting lyrically (like 'Bliss was it in that morn to be alive, And to be young was very Heaven') to some demotic sort of climax like this:

> Hope rose like a bird,
> Fear fell like its turd
> And all the waters were swinging
> And all the kings were in tatters
> When I was young.

Maybe I could incorporate it—a poem within a poem—in the Epilogue. But you see what I'm up against. As George Moore said, 'If you've been born a dactyl it's difficult to lead a spondaic life'. (George was never very good at metre, and Yeats must have been thinking of this on the occasion when he met O'Connor in the Dublin street. 'How are you, Yeats?' inquired O'Connor. 'Not very well, not very well,' said Yeats, 'I can only write prose today.')

Forgive this final delay: it'll be as brief, I promise you, as I can possibly make it, for I'm intent on meeting you and can't meet you without bringing something worth-while in my hand.

If we met again that year, he brought nothing in his hand. Had he done so, I doubt if the verses, which sound impromptu in his letter, would have survived his stern judgement. By August he was off to Pitzer College in Claremont, California, the last rainbow with the pot of gold, though iron pyrites for poets. I left him the winter to settle and then reminded him of Louis' memory, a still potent spell. On 6 February, 1967, he wrote, sanguine again. He would send the Epilogue in a week. 'I feel like a robin that has got mixed up in a badminton match.' He complained of popularity—his classes were too well attended by the young, which I could well believe.

To live and move and have your Boeing here, you would need (as an old Austrian friend used to say, referring to the Viennese women) a diesel in your bum, or at least in your elbow.' But he now had a secretary and he was going to write each month or fortnight about articles being revised for the book or replaced. 'For the first time in fifteen years I have steady and stated money coming in to me each month; I can hardly believe it, but it does mean I can plan ahead instead of being at the mercy of misfortune and of myself.

I hope what I've said will prove to be acceptable in the event. It can't make things worse and it may make them less bitter.

He was back for that summer in Colchester. Before he went to America he had written to John Hewitt: 'Louis, Spencer, Roethke, Burns-Singer, Brendan—most of them falling off the wires suddenly like October swallows who have been picked off by a delinquent teenage lad with a new air-gun.' Now his own turn was coming. In Colchester he fell ill and had two serious operations. I was desk-bound and did not see him till 20 December in London, the day before he was due to return to California.

We found him, my wife and I, nominally in bed, at the English-Speaking Union Club, Marianne unobtrusively in charge. He was spirited and cheerful, though frail. We drank whisky with water from the wash-basin. He sat up against his pillows and talked little of 'The Character of Ireland' and much of Ireland's characters. Old friends like Reggie Smith and Eric Ewens began to appear. It was not a saloon bar, but at least a saloon bed. For some reason we had to be back in Oxford by an earlyish train. We left him, smiling among friends. The thought suggested itself that we might not see him again. I did not accept it. So many had died now, but I was still not quite out of the stage where one expected everyone to turn up again.

He went off to California next day, intending to return, but never to return. There were one or two letters after that, and then his last letter to me, written on 14 January, 1969. 'I thought —and the doctor thought—that I had emerged successfully from the wood, but apparently not; two or three trees have been pacing me.' He was to have another operation next day, in Los Angeles Hospital. The letter went on to discuss the last stages of 'The Character of Ireland'. On 2 February we heard on the B.B.C. night news that he was dead. His last programme was done. In the words of John Hewitt's moving obituary sonnet, 'Now that wild creature is run down at last'.

Writing of an earlier and less Irish Parnell than ours, Oliver Goldsmith said: 'A poet, while living, is seldom an object sufficiently great to attract attention. When his fame is increased by time it is then too late to investigate the peculiarities of his disposition; the dews of the morning are past, and we vainly try to continue the chase by the meridian splendour.' I did not know Rodgers in the dews of his morning and he had all too little of time and fame for meridian splendour. Nor is this the place to try and follow the hare who runs through his poems and his prose as he ran through life, the hare hounded not only, like Francis Thompson, by heaven, but by the man himself, the hound in him and the god in him; that hare that hid in his 'Harvest Field':

> Listen! Listen! do you hear the hiss
> Of the scythe in the long grasses of your laughter?
> More is mowed than you know, for this
> Is Time's swathe, you are the one he's after.

But, reading again that desperate renewal of promises, the refrain of his later letters to me, I see that the problem of the Epilogue was central to himself. It was to have been his Summa. Into it were to have gone, all reconciled, the discrete percepts of that mosaic mind. The expatriate was to have come home; he was to have been able 'To make the past happen properly, as we want it to happen': the cat of thought and the mouse of guilt which his poem, 'The Trinity', could not reconcile were to have settled at last together in the self to which they were domestic. He had feared 'The Shadow of Doubt, that pick-pocket of conviction', yet had hoped, as his Magi on their journey hoped:

> There was nowhere they would not go, feast or fast,
> Slum or salon, bethel or brothel, if only at last
> And at least they could come to the truth and be blessed.

In that epilogue, there would no longer have been any para-dox in a Presbyterian parson's Europa and the Bull, Pan and Syrinx, Apollo and Daphne. The Greek, the Roman and the Orange, would have been harmonized in an art free as the ancients conceived it and able to comprehend Belfast and Dublin, Wapping, Colchester, and California. Mary Magdalen would have been the Virgin and there would have been an Ireland such as Wolfe Tone had imagined, where North and South could be one, when Catholics digging with the left foot and Protestants with the right would no longer dig one another's graves except in friendship, and where a new past could be created with room for priest and presbyter written large or small, a past with room in the same Irish mind for Carson and for Michael Collins.

Such a poem could not be written in this world, not even in the last refuge of California. The soil could not be removed from the soul till the soul was in the soil, and the bull-man could become a god only when the clod had closed over him. So now the Epilogue, like Robert Emmett's epitaph, cannot be written. Its imago lives only in the Utopia of his poem 'Neither Here Nor There', shimmering and beckoning, glimpsed in 'A spool of birds spinning on a shaft of air', whenever the sun burns 'through the meshes of rain'. It is echoed in 'the suck and slap of a spade in the wet clay', and keeps its last promise in our memory of that man of 'undertones, and hesitance, and haze' who has hidden at last in 'the safest place—the bosom of the enemy'.

EXPRESS

As the through-train of words with white-hot whistle
Shrills past the heart's mean halts, the mind's full stops,
With all the signals down; past the small town
Contentment, and the citizens all leaning
And loitering parenthetically
In waiting-rooms, or interrogative on platforms;
Its screaming mouth crammed tight with urgent meaning,
—I, by it borne on, look out and wonder
To what happy or calamitous terminus
I am bound, what anonymity or what renown.

O if at length into Age, the last of all stations,
It slides and slows, and its smoky mane of thunder
Thins out, and I detrain; when I stand in that place
On whose piers and wharves, from all sources and seas,
Men wearily arrive—I pray that still
I may have with me my pities and indignations.

1

WORDS

Always the arriving winds of words
Pour like Atlantic gales over these ears,
These reefs, these foils and fenders, these shrinking
And sea-scalded edges of the brain-land.
Rebutted and rebounding, on they post
Past my remembrance, falling all unplanned.
But some day out of darkness they'll come forth,
Arrowed and narrowed into my tongue's tip,
And speak for me—their most astonished host.

BEAGLES

Over rock and wrinkled ground
Ran the lingering nose of hound,
The little and elastic hare
Stretched herself nor stayed to stare.

Stretched herself, and far away
Darted through the chinks of day,
Behind her, shouting out her name,
The whole blind world galloping came.

Over hills a running line
Curled like a whip-lash, fast and fine,
Past me sailed the sudden pack
Along the taut and tingling track.

From the far flat scene each shout
Like jig-saw piece came tumbling out,
I took and put them all together,
And then they turned into a tether.

A tether that held me to the hare
Here, there, and everywhere.

THE PIER

Only a placid sea, and
A pier where no boat comes,
But people stand at the end
And spit into the water,
Dimpling it, and watch a dog
That chins and churns back to land.

I had come here to see
Humbug embark, deported,
Protected from the crowd.
But he has not come today.
And anyway there is no boat
To take him. And no one cares.
So Humbug still walks our land
On stilts, is still looked up to.

4

CONCERT HALL

Still as lizard on stone,
Whose colour skids from the eye
They sit with startled hearts
And watch the weasel-lean voice
Twisting its way, soft and deft,
Through the stuttering stones
Of notation, neat-footed,
Steel-tight and pistol-instant.

Thin and pauseless as wind
Threading through holes, and easy
As ice sliding on heat,
It flows piecelessly on,
The bold deliberate voice
Lovely as dolphins leaping
In caterpillar loops,
Quick as hawk flickering
Or swallow sweeping
Its whip-end over eaves,
Smooth as the water-ribbon
Brimming the slippy lip
Of the full mountain pool.

But jerked as broken stick,
Sudden as jagged spark,
It jumps from peak to peak
Of the high rocky air,
Till like ecstatic lark
Or rocket it reaches
Its last and topmost note.
And silence falls in the hall,
Like a fresh-gutted glove
That still retains the shape
Of the informing hand.

THE PARTY

So they went, leaving a picnic-litter of talk
And broken glitter of jokes, the burst bags of spite:
In comes Contempt the caretaker, eye on ceiling,
Broom in armpit, and with one wide careless cast
Sweeps the stuttering rubbish out of memory,
Opens the shutters, puts out the intimate lamp,
And, a moment, gazes on the mute enormities
Of distant dawn. And far doors bang in mind, idly.

WAR-TIME

Now all our hurries that hung up on hooks,
And all our heels that idly kicked in halls,
And all our angers that at anchor swung,
And all our youth long tethered to dole-lines,
And all our roots that rotted deep in dump,
Are recollected: in country places
Old men gather the children round them now,
As an old tree, when lopped of every bough,
Gathers the young leaves into itself, a frilled stump.

THEIR EXCELLENCIES

The stage of chivalry is gone,
Glib speech and predicated sob,
And now the cast we gaped upon
Is down and howling with the mob.

But still polite and obdurate
The high and hidden diplomats
Hold up the old back-drops and wait,
Like scene-shifters, dispassionate.

Above their heads unheeded clang
The hubbub bells of a new day,
Under their stony eyelids hang
The icicles of memory.

THE LOVERS

After the tiff there was stiff silence, till
One word, flung in centre like single stone,
Starred and cracked the ice of her resentment
To its edge. From that stung core opened and
Poured up one outward and widening wave
Of eager and extravagant anger.

THE FAR-OFF HILLS

It is a pity that distance puts
Ten-league boots on brutality,
That the glib spittle of steel claps down
Miles below, in a spidery splash,
On the pin-point town,
Gumming grimacing faces to the pavement,
While the alert executor, lark-light,
Tiny climber in titanic chasm,
Rinses the pin-prick pity in the burst
And cloudy roundabout of pride.

It is a pity that distance props
The deed of darkness bright side up,
That no round returning view
Rocks the airman's aim askew,
Implicates his blood and bone,
Makes another's wound his own,
Explodes the cool and grounded map
Of his airy purpose into angry domes
Of his own doom, resists and rusts the hand
That tears along the dotted lines of life.

It is a pity that distance releases us
From the quick retort, the tight resistance,
The press and prison of sanctioning wills,
Unseals the quivering and indriven heart
That in the burrows of imagination
Runs from the kennelled hound and hears the horn
Of tomorrow's hunt; distance enlarges it,
Lets loose the schoolboy to spit and jeer,
Lets loose the arrogant engineer,
Allows assault upon a serene people
And clangs death's bell in every heady steeple.

It is a pity that distance binds
Loose-leaf life into its narrow tome,
Poses the snarling waves in smiling line,

Freezes the flying foot to photographic stare,
Slurs all leaping syllables to one smooth smear,
Stilts us like gods, gives us vest-pocket views
Of Himalayan chaos and chameleon hues,
Fixes calm frames around the edgeless riot
—Until earth's scene grows shallow, and we stand
Only ankle-deep in its agony.

So we with windy and unweighed desire
Balloon our hero to vicarious height,
Hoop him with ceremony, hub him with awe,
Insulate him from remonstrance, sift his mail,
Dislink him from laughter and reason's ballast,
Till in the high and windless land he sits
Removed from tears, equipped with files and writs,
Each bell-push a man, each microphone a nation,
His glacial word carving the living riot
Into dead track and fearful fluent rut.

But tomorrow, perhaps, walking in the city,
Soothed by apt paths and habitual paces,
Sliding oiled eyes over the far-off hills
And foreign ills, or sitting in rooms,
Fitting, with cold tongs of reason and wit,
The hot hates and sticky loyalties
Of our day into jig-saw discussion
—O then will the abrupt bolt and naked shock
Shrink the glittering sheet of our laughter
Into tinfoil drops, and reinstate us
In our imagination and pity.

SING, BROTHERS, SING!

In cinemas we sought
The syrupy event,
In morning paper bought
Our cosy sentiment.

We eyed shop-windows packed
With leisured gun and rod
For the fastidious act
Of poking fun like God.

Each evening to amuse,
The radio-cage unveiled,
To speak the shocking news
The parrot never failed.

Its insulated tones
Reporting perfectly
Alarming war-zones,
The usual perfidy.

The bright and mirror voice
Reviewed the scrimmages,
Deleting heat and noise
From all its images.

Each evening it drew
A round-robin applause,
For it confirmed anew
Our own and Nature's laws.

At our back-door we failed to hear
War's dust-bin chariot drawing near.

SPRING

Rack upon rack of leaves all elbowing
From end to end of every bony wood,
And frill upon frill of water hanging
From hill to hill, and over all, in tiers,
The tiny shrapnel-bursts of song that hood
And hem the climbing lark tunnelling clear.

All the bells and hullabalooes of joy
Ring in the tingling flesh of bull and boy,
Everywhere in our loud and lighted land
The lewdest notions now make holiday,
Now on the least mouse-blink of nakedness
Pounces the lion, Lust. Limbs and lambs play.

Old lonely men lean back in limousines,
Miser-fingers locked on their bellies' purse,
Looking fixedly ahead as they slide
Silently on like shadows across screens
Past the Easter crowds banked up on pavements,
Waiting for a wedding, mobbing a bride.

END OF A WORLD

OLD MAN

Yes, in one night all the marble heroes
Came down from their high decks and marched away
Into anonymity like pierrots,
Our flags climbed down their own ropes like spiders
And scuttled off, also the tame salute
Went wild and flew away out of our hands,
Our roof of government slumped, and our laws
Slid like slates, unsettling everywhere,
Title's kite-string broke, and Rank's anchor sprang.
I could tell you a hundred happenings
Of that anxious night, I could recount how
Our social circus shook, angry cages burst,
The animal acts escaped and ran amok,
The lion-tamer Discipline was mauled,
Sentiment bitten by his own charmed snake,
The lariat Intellect lassoed itself,
And the sly Illusionist sought safety
In his own deceptions. And that wild pig
Contempt, poking in the heart's levelled drives
Of habit, and old holdings of desire,
Snooped out the pious wish and snouted up
The planted response. And, on top of that,
Scathing winds of hate came, bringing locusts
Which ate our fig-leaf sensitivity,
Our grass-skirt insularity and poise.
Freely our frozen loyalties thawed, and
An annulling flood suddenly straddled
All the lock-gates of class, caste, and custom,
All the sluices and allotted safeties
Of our civilization, all names, norms,
Numbers, paths, proprieties, all were drowned
In rebellion's mound of mounting waters.
And we who were warned, like Noah, floated
Upright on that sea, and saw the broken
Pieces of our old world bobbing past us,
Saw the contents of History's tied shops

Spread on the flood untidily, saw all
The bric-à-brac, the crates of government
Tumbled out, old boxes of tricks, ends, means,
Poses and properties, plumes, palliums,
Exact dignity, calculated awe,
The props and back-drops of authority
—We saw them all swept past us. There sprawled
The dead diplomat, inseparable
On his finger-end the skeleton keys
Of compromise and ambiguity.
There too floated the drowned scholar, his hand
Holding his pat reference and apt tag,
Index and document, his subscription
To Authority. There danced the landsman who
Collected sea-birds' eggs and sailors' slang,
The expert alpinist bed-rid from birth,
The strategist who never met his gun,
The record-keepers of record-breakers,
The lackers and onlookers of greatness,
Eunuch students of love and peeping Toms,
Caretakers of leapfrogging pedigrees
—All were there, all the tasters and testers
Of things rare, intricate, antique, lofty,
Exotic, difficult, all who had sieved
The theory from the practice, the fancy
From the fact, the seekers and abstractors
Of size, shape, surface, sound—all who kept pure
The exquisite equation of self, all
Fallen to pieces like a jogged jig-saw,
The end of a world witty and heartless.
And we, only, were left, a plain people
Without name or memory, lifted up
On the obliterating back of doom.

But floods divided, dropped and brought to view
A levelled world waiting to be made new.
Old hives were honeyless, bee-lines led nowhere,

15

Roads still ran, but only to link ruins,
No mat or footmark, glass or gaze,—eagles
Had picked the eyes and meaning out of maps.
Some, homesick for the fixed features, argued
That we would never find a way, would move
And wander on through featureless land
Looking for aims, as on some Arctic waste
The lost explorer moves, moored to sameness
Of snow, impossible to memorize,
No hook for eye, no hug for heart, no route
For foot, no return, no base. So they said.
But we took bearings with our high hopes' help,
Struck stakes out of our strict resolves, drove roads,
Found knowledge hidden in our needs,
Plotted new maps out of our own exploits,
Our thirsts sank wells, turned water into wine,
Our appetites caught food on the wing; we,
Not counting any wound we gave or got,
Ran past warnings, threw bridges over seas,
Or, impatient, walked on the water. Death
Times us. Our wills bounded lightly across
The single and yielding ledge of the moment,
We heard it falling behind us, but we
Looked not back. On that narrow road we strode
Straight forward to desire, stripped, not stopping
Or side-stepping into explanation.
No blow could dent us, or kiss relax us,
Or risk excuse us from our conclusion.
We shook off the detaining hands of friends,
Refused ease. Some said we were insensitive.
But no! At the heart's heat our putty thoughts
Had hardened into stubborn purposes,
And our hopes, so often lightly relaxed,
No longer now snapped back to apathy
But stayed stretched out to sticking-point, intent
On attainment. Until in every place,
Camp, court, clearing, meeting-ground, where once stood

Like tombstones the jacked-up effigies, plaques,
And rigorous monuments of Justice,
As reminders and remainders, just men
Walked; where Glory mildewed in medals
Or lurked in archives and excavations,
Men lived and laughed gloriously now,
The Word made flesh, melted into motion.

That, stranger, is my tale; learn from it how
Instantly an old world with ingrown eye
Engrossed in reflection, immobilized
In precedent, its body dropsical
With tradition, but poised and sprung on awe,
Fell. For the flood came, and in one night
The steep gradients of society,
Of luxury and lack, of fee and dole,
Slid, were levelled and laved. No doubt these would
Have waited till they were weathered away,
Or till hill lent hollow an impulsive hand.
But the flood laughed, and lo, the solid land
Flowed like sand before that thaw of heart and
Spate of hate, heaped high by hindrance. The heart
That hates has no halts, and no brakes except
Those of love. So do no idle talking
About greased and gradual changes or
An oiled, reasoned, and orderly advance,
Agreed instalments of progress. Know, now,
That an old world has no heart in moving,
It shifts, but only to retain its ease,
Adopts and adapts the new positions
But only to occupy them against
Newcomers, advancing only itself.
Yet I would say, and would say it to those
Who from the grandstand of dreams see themselves
Crashing through crowds to single glory,
Those who are stoics on their own estates
(Free to indulge themselves or to refrain),

Forgetting the hokers and the grimed stokers
Of their civilized gains—O I would warn,
Would warn all the godlike, the ogreish, the great,
That men who hate to live will live to hate,
Will live like maimed Samson, hugging his shame
For long years, but alert for the moment
That levelled himself and his lords under
One impending and humiliating thunder.

Stranger

Now that you have wrought your revolution,
Turned jungle into park, Jack into Jill,
Have tamed all the lions (except perhaps
A few left for tourists and for contrast),
Now that all are owners of this estate,
Suited and sated—do you not suspect
That this new skin is the integument
Of unamenable nature?—I mean
That if you strip this bright new world you'll get
The old black underwear of greed unchanged.

Old Man

O you are one of those mirror men who
Wave and weep goodbye to themselves leaving
On the train for Tomorrow, who point back
To the iron track of instinct, the tied train
Of events, the irreversible wheels
Of history, and so relax on cushions
Of excuse, forgetting that action
Is in your hands, and time under your feet,
And the engine answers for speed or stop.
The shadow on the future is your own
Unfocused fear, thrown prodigally;
And your doubts are the private detectives
Employed by your dislike, to make a case

Against change or choice. Will you not be warned?
O listen now! Doom strikes strictly as clocks!
Go home to your own land! it is late there, and
The fading day of safety involves you.
The rooks boil and bubble above the woods,
But will soon settle. Only the warplanes
Still stretch and strain the sky. Their auguries
Are against you and what you undertake.
Perhaps you will be warned, but I think not.
In this, as in other things, it happens
That there is no royal road to learning,
But only rote and toil, tears and lean years:
Seldom unto as dim eyes as yours arose
Indemnifying faith and further sight
Immediately. Yet do not doubt
That to your darkened towns and drowsy fields
Day will return, day with a lovelier face,
And voices, children's children's voices, will
Rejoice in the dew-washed and discharged air
Of tears. O let their laughter be your care,
And light will be the load you carry then.

PAIRED LIVES

Though to strangers' approach
(Like swing doors cheek to cheek)
Presenting one smooth front
Of summed resistance and
Aligned resentment, yet,
On nearer view note how,
At the deflecting touch
Of intervening hand,
Each in its lonely arc
Reaches and rocks inward
(Retires and returns
Immediately to join
The other moiety).
Each singly yields to thrust,
Is hung on its own hinge
Of fear and hope, and in
Its own reticence rests.

SUMMER HOLIDAYS

New every morning now the clerk docks off
Yesterday's desk-date, jerks back the needle
On duty's disc, and noses and slides on
Round the ingrowing ring and exact track
Of old tactics till the day's contracting
Circle ends, and suddenly the idle needle
Skids wildly into zig-zag freedom
And tidy tailspin, the clerk knocks off
Abruptly, buttoning-up his coat.

And later, no doubt, you will see him
Nosing and sliding in orderly line
Into pin-lighted cinema, being led
Alertly to allotted seat of ease,
Relaxing with eyes like asterisks,
Or note him standing in stadium rind,
Waiting for joy to be unconfined, wanting
The electric hare let loose to recapture
Its first fine careless rapture.

Even here at the day's convenient halt
And within its convolvulous ring
He has his own hugged track, his strangling string
Of ingrained act, his railed and ready ease;
And coiled in this roundabout and tail-chase
Of private scope and escape is ever
The spin of flesh on the spindle of bone
Concentring all, with its brute ambitions,
Its acute and terrible attritions.

But few look up to see or consider
This, the slack and screw of their happiness,
The economic claw, the heart's own flaw,
The ambient of mixed routine and rout,
Few look, except to the standing desk-date
(Their only shoremark) that notes and notches

21

Time's indivisibly-flowing miles,
That recognizes the returning tide,
That remembers the arriving traveller.

New every morning through a thousand streets
Life siphons into offices, and worms
Into old workings, yet the entombed man
Waiting behind the walled weeks hears always
The deliberate taps of time loudening
And the rescuing days drawing nearer,
Till at last hope opens and the gloom
Gapes like a bomb about him—holiday hands
Beckon him from far lands, urge his escape.

So out of pent city and inland pit
They nose and slide by easy rut and rail
To distant sea-edge, spreading boldly
On sand-dunes, or lolling on piers
(The leash-ends of land),
Or, in pairs, pacing slowly, posing as idlers
Till the last hill hides
Them, and they hurry deliberately
On to the Land's End and hilt's halt of heart's desire.

Longing to skip over the edge of scope
They look out all day at the far islands,
Or scan with glass the slipping distances
To where, bold in some enormous valley,
Walled and bottomed by the swinging water,
The cormorant squats; or between tide-lines
They march for miles searching for shells, leaping
Back when the swan-neck wave pours down and pounds
Out to yellow hissing beaks at their feet.

Here in these strange places no memory
Arrests and edits the running reel

Of their eager extravagant acts, fear
Lays no detaining or determining hand
On them, the backward light of precedent
No longer faces them with dutiful shadows
—Frolicking lives that at a finger's touch
Will curl like worms into a stiff conceit
And dead front of frightened consciousness.

Along the valley roads some roll in cars,
Looking for life on sky-lines, or in bars,
Mustered in bus on mystery trip they cheer
As the chartered miles gape before them
And zip obediently behind them,
Their fixed stare clattering like a stick
Across the sliding face and fence of fields
To the full stop where they interrogate
The great man's birthplace, or the rebel's grave.

Through bright gaps these sudden strangers snapshot
The slipshod landscape, and depart content.
But, coming home in the bare evening,
Memory on the mind's horizon edge
Like lightning prickles and flashes, and Care
Like caterpillar in curled leaf shrinks the heart,
For still the thread and threat of memory
Runs through these strange places and faces and
Jerks back the jumping beads of time and space.

And still from frugal bungalow and fig-leaf tent
The stockbroker, the stonebreaker, and the candlestick-maker
Trot into shop for morning newspaper,
Afraid to let the world go by without
Accommodating eye, anxious to acquaint
And equate their happiness with all
Unbalancing happenings, helplessly
Eager to follow the involving game
Or territorial noughts and crosses.

And still each night from alp and valley lap,
From all dividing individual aims
Life spokes into the town's sociable hub,
Where, under confetti-freckle of lights,
The girls in banana-bright bandanas
Parade down prickly lanes and lines of eyes;
Others round fun-stand wait the rocket-flash
Of wit on upturned faces, or applaud
The seal-like vocalist balancing one last note on voice-tip.

Far out on the wavering water they see
The pointed ship probe on to express end,
While they freely tonight at the slack edge
Of the vehement sea of affairs sit
And saunter; soon all must enter
That stiff and teeming centre tomorrow
Each homing heart released by time-table
Springs dove-like back to office ark and task, gives
One last elastic look and snaps away.

Away from outer rout to inner rut
And ironed route, away from the wild
And unwalled waste of wish, the zig-zag tracks,
The wilful freaks and fractures of habit,
The staccato acts of insurrection,
The guilty bed, the naked bathe, the night
Annexed from niggard eyes by drunkenness,
The lonely climb at dawn, all the jerky
Gap-toothed gamut of places and spaces.

Away from these eccentric ends to the city's
Centripetal calm and planetary core
Of custom and corporate act, away
To private lawns and privet lanes
With pilot kerbs and polite drains,
Day's slick pay-lines, night's slack play-pens
Where we are ticketed and trickled into

Stalls, and turnstiled into galleries and grades
And apt groups, like pebbles that elbow and
Rub shiny shoulders on a narrow beach.

—Thus on the round and turning stage of flesh
We present to you the usual act,
Rut and Rout, alias Butt and Rebut,
Alias Leash and Release, the magpie pair
In their bitter backbiting, ball-bouncing,
And reciprocating patter. No doubt
You have seen it before, for it is
The same yesterday, today, and for ever,
Showing at all houses and theatres,
The skeleton of all our furbished plays.

For not by gradual stealthy steps do we
Move onwards to a plotted destiny,
But between antimonies we are stretched
And pent, and catapulted to new ends
And angry issues. Note, now, how in us
Each thing resists and buoys its opposite,
Goodness is foreskinned and frisked by Evil,
And Violence advances Reason's forces,
Cruelty recruits Kindness, and titan
Dictators tickle tom-tit democrats.

And Faith beats down the enemy's last gate,
But listless then with resistless halls
Dies of its enemy's death; thus do you see
The saw-toothed graph drawn daily, inking
The in-and-out of action, linking rut and rout,
But few look up to know, few seek to master
These see-saw forces until disaster
Breaks the pithless sticks of apathy, and then
Through gaps of anger heady droves will hurry
And into panic-traps hot hooves will huddle.

And what will be left of us then but our faces
In albums, our names on war's memorials,
Our number on old disc picked up by peasant?
History's putty shapes, pitied or praised
According to public mode or private mood,
We have done it ourselves and need expect
No less, for the music goes round and round
In the old rings, new every morning,
The spin of flesh on the spindle of bone
Concentring all, with its brute ambitions,
Its acute and terrible attritions.

THE RAIDER

There, wrapped in his own roars, the lone airman
Swims like a mote through the thousands of eyes
That look up at him ironing out the skies,
Frocked and fanged by fire, by nagging fingers
Of guns jagged and jogged, with shell-bursts tasselled.

Does ever the airman's eye, speeding on
To grim conclusion, alight and loiter
Curiously on the country below?
Or does his gaze easily dissolve
Upon the moving surfaces, and flow
Evenly away like rain on rivers?

Or, roaring back over our armoured rims,
Does his mind take in only the bloom and boom
Of bomb beneath him, noting how neatly
It mopped up a map-point town or snouted out
This tip or else that tap-root of resistance?

Yet, pity him too, that navigator
Who now in archipelago of steel
Nears that place where, hooked upon barbed air, he'll
Halt, hang hump-backed, and look into his crater.

SUMMER DAY

But, heedful of the man who walks alone
On the dunes now at noon, in the heat here
At the sightless bottom of a sand-bowl
Two lovers hesitate, stop, looking up
At the single eye of sky vacantly
Accusing them, at the stiffened ashes
Of grasses circling it. But nothing moves.
And they again resume their easy grooves.

AN IRISH LAKE

There in the hard light
Dark birds, pink-footed, dab and pick
Among the addery roots and marrowy stones,
And the blown waves blink and hiccup at the lake's
Lip. A late bee blares and drones on inland
Into a cone-point of silence, and I
Lying at the rhododendron's foot
Look through five fingers' grille at the lake
Shaking, at the bare and backward plain, and
The running and bending hills that carry
Like a conveyer belt the bright snail-line
Of clouds along the sky all day unendingly.

There, far from the slack noose of rumour
That tightens into choking fact, I relax,
And sound and sights and scents sail slowly by.
But suddenly, like delicate and tilted italics,
The up-standing birds stretch urgently away
Into the sky as suddenly grown grey.
Night rounds on Europe now. And I must go.
Before its hostile faces peer and pour
Over the mind's rim enveloping me,
And my so-frightened thoughts dart here and there
Like trout among their grim stony gazes.

ACTION STATION

Evil, that was once the twisted gut
Of feeling in me, giving no ease
Or egress to the heart, making it
Ache with thought, and holding it inert
And introvert, locked and rotted with
Inaction, is now no longer that.

Not now are the private avenues
Of feeling contained and occluded,
Not now are our houses our prisons,
Or our hugged opinions oppressive,
And not at the suffocating fire
Of ventless faith do we sit and weep.

War shot its spark, and our shut chimneys
Shed and vehemently vomited
Their woolly volumes. From our hearts' hearths,
Past the dampers, checks, and private chokes
And sooted flues of feeling, issued
In ashy sheets the shy repressions.

For Evil is now overt and aloof,
And not in our selves but in our skies
And on our seas opposes the ease
Of our omnibus body. Look how
All the lines of our lives converge on
The gun's focus and the bullets' fan.

STORMY DAY

O look how the loops and balloons of bloom
Bobbing on long strings from the finger-ends
And knuckles of the lurching cherry-tree
Heap and hug, elbow and part, this wild day,
Like a careless carillon cavorting;
And the beaded whips of the beeches splay
And dip like anchored weed round a drowned rock,
And hovering effortlessly the rooks
Hang on the wind's effrontery as if
On hooks, then loose their hold and slide away
Like sleet sidewards down the warm swimming sweep
Of wind. O it is a lovely time when
Out of the sunk and rigid sumps of thought
Our hearts rise and race with new sounds and sights
And signs, tingling delightedly at the sting
And crunch of springless carts on gritty roads,
The caught kite dangling in the skinny wires,
The swipe of a swallow across the eyes,
Striped awnings stretched on lawns. New things surprise
And stop us everywhere. In the parks
The fountains scoop and flower like rockets
Over the oval ponds whose even skin
Is pocked and goosefleshed by their niggling rain
That frocks a naked core of statuary.
And at jetty's jut, roped and ripe for hire,
The yellow boats lie yielding and lolling,
Jilted and jolted like jellies. But look!
There! Do you see, crucified on palings,
Motionless news-posters announcing
That now the frozen armies melt and meet
And smash? Go home now, for, try as you may,
You will not shake off that fact today.
Behind you limps that dog with tarry paw,
As behind him, perfectly-timed, follows
The dumb shadow that mimes him all the way.

ESCAPE

The roads of Europe are running away from the war,
Running fast over the mined bridges and past the men
Waiting there, with watch, ready to maim and arrest them,
And strong overhead the long snorings of the planes' tracks
Are stretching like rafters from end to end of their power.
Turn back, you who want to escape or want to forget
The ruin of all your regards. You will be more free
At the thoughtless centre of slaughter than you would be
Standing chained to the telephone-end while the world cracks.

DIRECTIONS TO A REBEL

Keep away from roads' webs, they always lead
To some spider-spot where, once spied, out-speeds
The cop. Side-step the strict keepers of paths,
The pickets of prerogative; avoid
Conforming pass-word. But follow freely
The treeless plain of candour where shadows
Cannot hide or walk upright. Keep downwind;
Beware the water-hole of Want, for there
The hunter waits with widespread net of dole
And charity to take and tame you in
(Observe his footmark firm in the meek muck
Of softness and servility). Do not
On the taut returning tether of self
Dally and circle, nor in pond explore
Your rare reflection, stopping and stooping.
Stride straight on, stay stretched out, anticipate
No respite. And let neither friend's defect
Nor foe's respect divert you. On your way
You will pass horrible warning corpses
Wrecked on the hairpin-bend of reaction:
Beyond the burning town of Sloth you'll see
The hopeless citizens look back in tears
Salt pillars of self-pity, silhouettes
Of blank regret. But waste no word on them,
Go your way. Overhead, Fear and Favour,
The twin engines of Authority, will
Fill and fan your ears with their roaring. Scorn
Will curl suddenly round silent corners
Like bell-less bicycles: and Luxury
Draw up beside you, offering a seat
Moss-soft in idle limousine; foot-sore,
Refuse it. Marginal misgivings lie
In ambush. Crooked fingers will beckon,
Insistent strangers take you by the hand,
Dub you as friend, and plant their guilty coins
In unsuspecting pocket. So be you
Thorned and thicketed in reticence.

Make no loose friends: shun the too-nimble man
Who from being the heels of the hunted
Becomes the head of the hunter; be warned
Against the merchant who inflates and tags
His goods with flattery, or cellophanes
And surfaces his own self-interest
With saving and transparent honesty,
Who offers you his watertight word
Backed by his wickerwork act. Above all,
Beware the welcoming word on mat
Inviting the confiding footfall on;
Often it is stretched on slipperiness:
Avoid the hearty and enhancing handshake,
The prefatory fib that leads to worse
(Like gladiators' kisses, boxers' hugs,
The formal overtures to violence).
Accept no candid or contingent gift
From an ambiguous hand, or else like cog
You must have intercourse with ill and will
Be geared to new and necessary wrong.
Rise from table! rush from hall! O do not
Acquiesce in their toadying truths, refuse
To sing their subsidized praises, or borrow
Their easy loans; those are the open traps
For apathy: boot and batter them. Be
Intolerant, not backward to applaud
But forward to condemn, giving no ease.
May no insolent stone turn back your step,
No sea-blow dent your boat, no landfall
End your voyage. Elbowed from port to port,
Signalled from point to point, drop no anchor;
Seek no safe caves or tied and tidy coves.
Let not lax beds or luxurious hugs hold
Or detain you. The harbour gapes, but not
For you; arms open, but they are not yours.
Along your road you will meet no great crowds
Going with gongs to greet you returning

With your gains to an ungrudged conclusion.
Only expulsion, obloquy, and shame
Watch for you. Welcome them. Welcome too
Smooth malice, smarmy enmity, these things
Will shape and sharp your purpose, stroke and strop
Your temper, point your passionate aim. So,
Gay in the midst of growling things, you'll go
Tip-toe, songs in your ears, sights in your eyes,
That blind and deafen you to compromise.

THE INTERNED REFUGEE

And I was left here in the darkened house,
Listening for the fat click of the softly-shut door,
Looking for the oiled glint and ghost of light
Sliding soundlessly along the wall toward me,
Knowing that round me They were mobilizing
Their cold implacable forces slowly.

I shouted and none answered, one by one
My listening hopes crept back to me
Out of that dead place; mine was a lighted face
Looking into darkness, seen, but seeing nothing.

SNOW

Out of the grey air grew snow and more snow
Soundlessly in nonillions of flakes
Commingling and sinking negligently
To ground, soft as froth and easy as ashes
Alighting, closing the ring of sight. And,
Silting, it augmented everything
Furring the bare leaf, blurring the thorn,
Fluffing, too, the telephone-wire, padding
All the paths and boosting boots, and puffing
Big over rims, like boiling milk, meekly
Indulging the bulging hill, and boldly
Bolstering the retiring hole, until
It owned and integrated all. And then
Snow stopped, disclosing anonymity
Imposed, the blank and blotless sea in which
Both dotted tree and dashing bird were sunk,
And anchored ground and rocking grass engrossed.

And soon the knock and hiss of cistern ceased as
Gradually with inklings and wrinkling strings
Of ice the thickening cold anchored the skin
And slow core of water, gluing and glossing
All leaks, niggling or great, naked or guarded.
Long snaughters of ice at the tap's snout hung
Jagged and stiff like straw-ends this hard morning.
At every vent things hesitated; here,
In conforming holes and huts, the shy creatures
Shrank from issuing, and, rooted together,
Stood arrested and irresolute at doors,
Peppering with peepings the surprising fields—
Fox in knoll, fowl in house, heifer in hovel.
Only the bull, dubious and delicate, stalked
In his paddock, distrust spiking his blind steps.
His spinning eye, his spoked glances, glinted and
Tilted. His horn gored and scorned the ground, and scored
The oak, and fans of vapour jetted and jumped
Stiffly from nostrils, incensing the loose snow

Like smoke, and powdering his knees. Noisily
On the sleeked lake onlookers lingered in ring
Round the single and deferent skater lean-
      ing over in flight, like grass slanted by wind,
Foot-engrossed, locked in his own looking-glass
Of conscious joy and evident finery
Of movement, forgetful of outer voices.
Forgetful of venom, of fame, of laughter,
Of flouting Evil and of touting Good that
Waited woodenly for him like tormentors
At the end and edge of his dream, to waken
And claim him. So he slid on, as we all do,
Forgetting the morrow, forgetting too
The marrow of water in the bone of ice
(Like the worm in the wood), the liquefaction
And friction in all fixed things, virtue in vice,
The bomb domanial in the dome of blue.

WHITE CHRISTMAS

Punctually at Christmas the soft plush
Of sentiment snows down, embosoms all
The sharp and pointed shapes of venoms, shawls
The hills and hides the shocking holes of this
Uneven world of want and wealth, cushions
With cosy wish like cotton-wool the cool
Arm's-length interstices of caste and class,
And into obese folds subtracts from sight
All truculent acts, bleeding the world white.

Punctually that glib pair, Peace and Goodwill,
Emerges royally to take the air,
Collect the bows, assimilate the smiles,
Of waiting men. It is genial time.
Angels, like stalactites, descend from heaven,
Bishops distribute their own weight in words,
Congratulate the poor on Christlike lack,
And the member for the constituency
Feeds the five thousand, and has plenty back.

Punctually tonight, in old stone circles
Of set reunion, families stiffly sit
And listen; this is the night, and this the happy time
When the tinned milk of human kindness is
Upheld and holed by radio-appeal.
Hushed are hurrying heels on hard roads,
And every parlour's a pink pond of light
To the cold and travelling man going by
In the dark, without a bark or a bite.

But punctually tomorrow you will see
All this silent and dissembling world
Of silted sentiment suddenly melt
Into mush and watery welter of words
Beneath the warm and moving traffic of
Feet and actual fact. Over the stark plain

The stilted mill-chimneys once again spread
Their sackcloth and ashes, a flowing mane
Of repentance for the false day that's fled.

MUSIC IN WAR-TIME

All things, even our thoughts' shapes, subscribe
To these importunate times. Like bomb
The impending baton drops, impacts
And detonates in pancake-clap
The unanimous instruments.
And from sunk pit the upstart trumpet
Juts and jets jumpily like gun. See
How the lean violins dive and flow
In close formation, or swerve suavely
In felt line, all weaving and waving
Interminably to and fro,
Whirling and wheeling and whorling
Like aerial convoy combating
Round the heavy and sonorous theme
That snores and snouts steadily on.
Or through the throbbing dark the oboe
Probes and throws its thin blue bore of light
Reflectively far into the night.
Or mark, there amid the sounding swim
And swirled expanse, opposed and taut,
An alien phrase up-pokes and breaks
Tentatively like periscope
Scanning the circular surface,
The ominous drum drops its depth-charge,
Arrests the racing tide of music.
While steadily underneath, the sweeps
Of counterpoint search the sea-satchels,
Combing through the thoughtless unknown deeps
A clear and harmonious lane-way
For following and conducted ears.

IRELAND

O these lakes and all gills that live in them,
These acres and all legs that walk on them,
These tall winds and all wings that cling to them,
Are part and parcel of me, bit and bundle,
Thumb and thimble. Them I am, but none more
Than the mountains of Mourne that turn and trundle
Roundly like slow coils of oil along the shore
Of Down and on inland. When I begin
To draw my memory's nets and outlines in,
Then through its measured mesh escapes the fuss
And fluster of all the finicky things.
Of the Mournes I remember most the mist,
The grey granite goosefleshed, the minute
And blazing parachutes of fuchsia, and us
Listening to the tiny clustered clinks
Of little chisels tinkling tirelessly
On stone, like a drip of birds' beaks picking
Rapidly at scattered grain. I think of those
Wet sodden days when we, for miles and miles,
Steadily padded the slow sponge of turf
That squealed and squelched cold between our bared toes;
Or on airy ridge, urgent and agile, ran,
A chain of jigging figures on the sky-line;
Or skilfully in file, followed, tricking
The hoops of hairy bramble in our path,
Poking in undergrowth and picking
The bitter berries that prickle the springs
Of the dark mouth. There was Bloody River
Where the granite pickles bristled and blazed, and
Ebullient water bellied over
Boulders with the sweep of a bell's shoulders,
And pancaked out in pools: Drinihilla
Where the gales smoothed and glued back the eyelids:
The granite river that is called Kilkeel,
Whose beds were clean and gritty like oatmeal:
And Commedagh in whose high summer heat
Nothing stirred, only the shimmering bleat

Of sheep; and we, as we sat and chattered,
Marked the motionless shine of falls far-off
On Binyon, and nothing at all mattered:
And Legawherry so soft and grassy,
Where the white scuts lazily scattered,
And never in their remotest burrows
Did ferret-Fear come closely after them:
Slieve-na-brock and its long pig-tail trickles
That hung down the bald rocks, reaching to
The glossy backs of the bracken. And Donard
Where, high over all hanging, the strong hawk
Held in his eyes whole kingdoms, sources, seas,
And in his foot-hooks felt all things wriggling
Like the single string of river niggling
Among the enormous mountain bottoms.
Bearnagh and Lamigan and Chimney-Rock,
Spelga, Pulgarve, and Cove—all these names lie
Silently in my grass-grown memory,
Each one bright and steady as a frog's eye;
But touch it and it leaps, leaps like a bead
Of mercury that breaks and scatters
Suddenly in a thousand shining strings
And running spools and ever-dwindling rings
Round the mind's bowl, till at last all drop,
Lumped and leaden again, to one full stop.

THE FOUNTAINS

Suddenly all the fountains in the park
Opened smoothly their umbrellas of water,
Yet there was none but me to miss or mark
Their peacock show, and so I moved away
Uneasily, like one who at a play
Finds himself all alone, and will not stay.

TO THE PREACHER

You suck in Good,
And spit out Sin
Just as you would
A spent grape-skin.

Light as a glove
You separate
The thing you love
From that you hate.

But this divorce
And glib conclusion
Is got, of course,
By their collusion.

In you contend
Both Good and Ill,
This will not end
In final spill

Of one or other:
God is not mocked, for
In steps Bother,
The King's Proctor.

WORDS

Once words were unthinking things, signalling
Artlessly the heart's secret screech or roar,
Its foremost ardour or its farthest wish,
Its actual ache or naked rancour.
And once they were the gangways for anger,
Over-riding the mind's qualms and quagmires,
Wires that through weary miles of slow surmise
Carried the feverish message of fact
In their effortless core. Once they were these.
But now they are the life-like skins and screens
Stretched skilfully on frames and formulae
To terrify or tame, cynical shows
Meant only to deter or draw men on,
The tricks and tags of every demagogue,
Mere scarecrow proverbs, rhetorical decoys,
Face-savers, salves, façades, the shields and shells
Of shored decay behind which cave-minds sleep
And sprawl like gangsters behind bodyguards.

Today walk down the two-way street of words
(Past the empty shop-fronts of abstraction
In which everyone views his own loved face),
Often you'll see the window-dressing man
Emerging to admire his own effect
Of touting talk and taking images,
Observe his dummy topics draped with speech,
His spaced and studied periods. See how
To snobs he offers the exclusive phrase,
And to mobs the one extensively worn.
But go your way, nor envy the rich man
His bought and polished phrase like limousine
That waits outside his door obediently.
Go your way, for every road and rail
Leads to the Fun-Fair of Words, there, chum with
The charmed and chiming folk who crowd forward
Offering their faces as mirrors, their ears
As echoes for their favourite showmen

And their shams. Note on every sky-line
And headline, hoist and husting, stilt and stall,
The tricky-of-tongue gesticulating,
The wheedling hawkers, the adroit talkers
Who in the give-and-take of argument
Ring the changes. See too the Demagogue
Strike his stance, hurl his hook, cast his query.
The Orator perform his strip-tease act
Of revealing candour and downright speech
With haste and stimulating hesitance
To greedy ears that gape for quick climax,
For that fine moment when the cloaked whisper
Is bared to showy shout. Observe the Preacher,
Dare-devil, who grim on his jacked-up car roars
Fearlessly through all the gears and gamut
Of godliness. Remark the journalist
With cliché like a weather-cock or cork
Always on top. Spy the vendor of puffs
Inflating his flat wares with epithet.
Gape at the parliamentary debate
Compèred and prim, the Punch-and-Judy show
Of calculated anger, rehearsed blows,
Predictable defeat. Laugh brazenly,
Embarrass the bold charlatan who will
Cry 'heads' when challenged, spin his partial coin
(Both sides a head) impressed with Patriotism.
Try your luck with books, chance the lucky dip,
Lose on the loaded dice of sentiment,
Let yourself go, swing on antithesis,
Switchback on rhythm, see-saw on awe and air,
Or travel miles on the merry-go-round
Of gossip. Gasp your fill, be intrigued by
The performing flea of precocity;
Listen to the medicine-man's patter
And buy his patent bottle of water;
Step smartly on the floor of irony,
Smear your anger with a laugh when you fall;

Enter the intimate tent, indulgently
Smile at the Oldest Word in the World, still
In perfect moving order, but unused.
Squint through the crooked gun-sights of your youth,
Hit the bull's-eye of truth and ring the bell
Of your elders' rattled astonishment.
Or try your skill at the queered quoits of wit,
Flinging on square peg the round hole of pique;
Test your strength by tugging the anchored weight
Of the academies (your money back).
O be thrilled by the death-defying dive
Of immortal words into a shallow bath
Of bathos. Visit the purple passage,
Exclaim at the magic touch. O strange things,
Today wait to tickle and intrigue you
In this Fun-Fair of Words tackle them all;
Snigger at parrot-talk; view, safe in cage,
The ape Pornography; engross yourself
In the monkey-words' style and appearance
But ignore what they are doing (sift Form
From Matter); consult the flattering voice
Behind the portentous curtain of Art,
Admire the mirror's faithfulness, admit
The palmist's skill. And before you depart,
Applaud the breathless exhibitionist
Throwing up his string of questions like quick balls
And catching all the answers coming down.
Watch the boneless wonder who can wriggle
Out of his rope of hard-and-fastened oath.
Be awed by that rare man who is able
To eat his own fiery words, and swallow
His sword-thrusts. Pity the stolid clown who
Sticks out his tongue's rocky peninsula
Into the rocking sea of raillery.
Look how on the tight-rope of decorum
The ambiguous word balances and
Tilts perilously, titillating us,

48

But instantly reverts to vertical.
Gaze gravely in the world's distorting glass,
Laugh at the skinny notice of your birth,
Or roar at your obese obituary.
O do the usual things, use the usual phrase—
Go the rounds, throw caution to the winds,
Taste life to its full, drink to excess, then,
When night falls, go home and vomit your fill.
Fiercely, fiercely say to yourself:
'O for a day when words will no longer be
Fig-leaves and frills for eunuchs, jingle-bells,
The bark subtracted from the biting dog,
The plywood surfaces of platitude
Politely hiding the hearts' hollow minds.
O for a world where words would always be
The windows of feeling (and not mere blinds),
Revealing and relieving living needs.
And that I could,
Looking from this between-times meeting, see
The cumbered evening leave, bare morning come
Leaping so clean, peeled clear of cloudy speech,
Morning more candid and abstemious
Of tongue, not touted nor convoyed
By crowds of toadying words, from mouthy claims exempt.
Soon may it come, and leave
My days all full of calm and empty of contempt.

AWAKE!

Wind that speeds the bee and plucks the bee-line
Into bows and bends, that clips the spoken word
From the open lips, that claps and batters
The bent-backed and running roaring waters,
That squats and squints and squeals evilly in trees,
That follows and faces the fleeing leaves,
That with hag hands hugs the hooked hawk down,
That hammers like rams' heads the humped body,
And that stamps flat like stallions the shaking
Flaking acres of grass—wind nine times named,
And by these wordy welts nine times inflamed
In mind—O mount now and mightily suck
Up all rooted breath out of the rotted mouth
Of man, collapse his plots and exploits, pluck
Every gut taut with terror, like weed
Tugged tight in withdrawing wave, and heedless
In high hangars hoard one blast, pack one breath.
Then fall, walled wind, all welded and one, clap
Wieldy water, scap, and valley gap
Together, and detach man from his map;
O wind, have no pity on the city
With buttery motto and lean dole-line
Like old tapeworm in its intestined street,
Or on the foreign laughter of those who boot
Through orchard pasted under foot with fruit,
Seek, suck, sack such, in each socket set tooth,
High over hoardings hurl, and all ways spill,
Hug the elbowing horde, hard under hill
Huddle hare and hound, let lion and lamb
Lump panic-struck, yoke in one choking hold
Victor and victim, rock trigger and target.
And O, halt our hates, file flat our flights,
With stiff pointed finger stuff and stifle
Every gaping gun and pouting rifle;
Pour over our floors and frontiers and leave
Pavement and field clean and ceiling clear,
And man, like Noah afloat in his ark

On a single sea, looking for landmark,
His heart's scope not yet shrunken into
Private and poisonous pools of feeling.

Alas! Æolus will not listen to
Our lot. No upright God angry and stiff
Will suddenly come turning somersaults
Of mercy and cartwheels of leniency
Toward us Noahs. Nor will words rock or wring,
Or invocation sting. At our appeal
No pulse will leap up like a bell-clapper
Proclaiming peace. To us no Nereus will
Rise from the ring of the sea like a rod,
His hair set and salty as dulse, bringing
Succour and promise. So spare your protests.
There are no interlopers in our fate.
Be sure of this, that in peace or war, we
Are where we are because of what we are:
No censor can excerpt, or scissor-snip
Excise this salient sentence from our lives.
O easy and peaceful were those days when
Our hopes bowled on before us like hoops,
And our biddable purposes pedalled
Slowly on rolling gradients of reason
And reform. Fools! in our stinking ditches
War was born, and grew gigantic legs that
Suddenly kicked the ground away like a frog
From under us all. For that is how
The world moves, not with meant and maintained pace
Toward some hill-horizon or held mood,
But in great jags and jerks, probed and prodded
From point to point of anger, exploded
By each new and opposed touch. So War came,
The late and urgent agent of Change, not
Of Chance. So will it always come to wake
The deep sleepers. See how its sudden hands
Now garter and grow round us like quicksands

Here in these islands. O awake! awake!
And let us like the trapped intrepid man
Who on prairie hears the holocaust roar
And sees his horizons running to meet him
In mutinous flames, while the still grasses fill
With rills of refugees, let us calmly
Stand now to windward, and here at our feet
Stooping, light fires of foresight that will clean
And clear the careless ground before us
Of all the dry and tindery increment
Of privilege. So will that other Fate
Arriving find no hold within our state,
And we on our ringed ground its roar will wait
Freely. Awake! before it is too late.

LIFE'S CIRCUMNAVIGATORS

Here, where the taut wave hangs
Its tented tons, we steer
Through rocking arch of eye
And creaking reach of ear,
Anchored to flying sky,
And chained to changing fear.

O when shall we, all spent,
Row in to some far strand,
And find, to our content,
The original land
From which our boat once went,
Though not the one we planned.

Us on that happy day
This fierce sea will release,
On our rough face of clay,
The final glaze of peace.
Our oars we all will lay
Down, and desire will cease.

EUROPA AND THE BULL

TO M

Come, Love; warm and widen me
From what I am to what I'll be.

Va dunque, e fa che tu costui ricinghe
  d'un giunco schietto, e che gli lavi il viso
  sì che ogni sucidume quinde stinghe:

chè non si converria l'occhio sorpriso
  d'alcuna nebbia andar davanti al primo
  ministro, ch'è di quei di Paradiso.

Questa isoletta intorno ad imo ad imo,
  laggiu, colà dove la batte l'onda,
  porta de' giunchi sopra il molle limo.

Null' altra pianta, che facesse fronda
  o indurasse, vi puote aver vita,
  però che alle percosse non seconda.
                    PURGATORIO, *Canto I*.

EUROPA AND THE BULL

Naked they came, a niggling core of girls
Magotting gaily in the curling wool
Of morning mist, and careless as the lark
That gargled overhead. They were the root
Of all that writhing air, the frothing rock
Of that grey sea in whose vacuity
Footless they stood, nor knew if it or they
Were moving now. Yet, even as they gazed,
Cave after cave of light calved out of gloom,
Roof rose on roof, laugh laddered into laugh
As on they glided through the muddling veils
Into the motionless meadow, clear as stone,
Interminably domed.
Nothing supernal here; only cow-parsley:
Any place was convenient velvet,
And everywhere was peace, pin-drizzled by
Bird-song; the bay bare like a gong
Unbruised. Easy at the sea's edge the rocks
Breathed up and down. The inland hills stood still
Like hoardings to be stared at. Happy place!
And happy happy day! How giddily then
They sleeked along the sand with smoking heels.
Some frayed off with fountain-fling of arms
To play and plunge, staccatoing the water
And some more slowly followed, picking the deep flowers
Out of the fume and underdrone of bees: green-kneed
They rose and fell in waves delightedly: new sights
Consumed them; new mites and motes of smell
Held and incensed them: crumbs of booty glowed
In every foot-dent, eiderdowntrodden.
And all among them moved the moon-like cows
Grazing light tracks across the long night-grass.
But look! the Bull! indubitably bull,
Elbowing slowly through the obeisant herd,
Blazing and bellowing. His massy head,
Laden like a dahlia, dallied and swung,
And his vast eye slid to and fro as sharp

57

And glaucous as sea-holly, salting all
Their thoughts with suddenness. They hardly knew
What most to admire: but most his hub of power
And circumambience of gentleness
Delighted them. Arms curved and craved to stroke
His milky sides, insidiously veined
With watery blues and bloody ivyings.
But how describe him? words can only add
To lightning the thunder's redundancy.
He was most godlike and most temperate.

Slow, slow, slow, with bubble-pause and slide
He paced before Europa there, and she
As if with shivering drew her shoulders now
Shyly about her, yet she shivered still.
Never did shadow so shimmer with midges
As she with switherings. Should she go?
Or no? Body and soul see-sawed in her.
As slowly the swan comes forward, in advance
Bearing its bellying tray of effusive plumes,
Yet backward rears its head and huffs its glance
As if it fended off its offering that presumes:
Swollen with slowness and undertowed by longing
It grows on the water, close, thundery, and thronging,
Till suddenly beside us, without fuss,
Immense it blossoms like a cumulus—
So slowly rose Europa, slowly she
Opened her fan-like self and mounted him
And spread her valances.
O how his reticence reined and trounced him then,
Lifting his feet into flounces of flight
And ratchet-edges of agitation,
Chawing each gentle step. To have and to hold—
How he would love to have but feared to hold
Her who as smooth as metal sat and smiled.
And how his silver slaverings flowed, and now
His chattering hooves danced under him like stones.

                              No one noticed
The Bull and Europa sloping away
Westward into the weed, she with both hands
Holding her bellyful of jolted joy,
Buoyant but dubious: he, bushed in stealth,
Tiptoadying tenderly, picking his way
Between brusque grass and briar, till at last
He waded out: the slow subtracting depths
Rose up; boldly he chinned the ruffling wave,
And wide the lifting side-cloths flowed, and fast
He mowed the watery swathes. She idly sat
Watching his knife-like knees divide and slide,
Slide and divide: only the hissing silks
Susurrous foamed about her.
Far from mainland and manland they swam,
Past many an island shawled and shimmering
In haze. The antlered trees stood still to gaze
At the amazing sight. On the shores
A thousand doors opened needle eyes
To take their thready beauty.
And O the mowers marching in the meadows,
And O the lowing cows. Still they swam on
Into the silent noon and ambience
Of sea so vast they hardly seemed to move
On its grave glass: its same and lazy glaze
Moored them everywhere. Still her eyes
Slid in their slotted cells, and still she searched
The satchels under her. There in a green night
The cloudy fish sailed by, too thin
To have a shadow, too light to have a stay.
And there were wandering veils that bellied up
And ebbed like blushes. Thready shapes of breath
Mouthed once, and went unsaid as innuendos
Under the stones. And O the blowing glooms
And overtones, the many streams that bore
From floor to floor the shining minnow-shoals
In rainbow rows that tore the smoky mane

With fire. Dug upon dug, tug upon tug
Of beauty fed Europa, till at last
She clapped her eyes and sang—

In what melodious mould
Was first this body rolled,
How was it overwashed
By winds, what rainbows lashed
Its eyes, what musics conched its ears,
What cataracts it broke
And tore to tags and smoke
That slowly wore it round and smooth as weirs,
And woods, too, grew in it, and volleys
Of finches flashed in all its valleys.
Only in soil the soul
Grows, and is coarsely whole,
For spirit has its commonplace and base;
Four seas conferred to build,
Four seasons too fulfilled
This body's scope, and gave it meaning and grace
Till from its bottle-loins there sprang
A hissing head and rocket-fang
Of life whose spittle drooped and spread
Its silver drivellings overhead,
Breaking the cold and middle ceiling,
And heavens hymeneal and farther-off revealing.

Night opened its slow and pinholed awning now
Over the sea. A slow and deferent fog
Rose up and fawned on them. evasively
Lolling its different tongues eleven ways
Like any dog.
No light, no light, but only separate depths
Of darkness glowed about them. Choked voices spoke.
And noiseless currents nosed and pulled like muscles
Their pleats of water tight. The bull swam on,
Hard and regardless. And gradually her hands

Like hyacinths curled closely in his hair;
Sometimes she clapped and palmed the patient brute
For very fear, and felt his ready pulse
Gulp like a bell. Until at last the compliant moon
Opened its pith and path of threadiness
Before their rush. In that green rind and round
Of sea its peeled stripe sprang invitingly
Single and taut between them and their goal,
And fast they flashed along it. Hour after hour
The rhyming furrows met them, sweetly-timed
And chiming to their mood; hour after hour
Miming the dipping dolphin-backs that swelled
And fell in swathes; slide and divide, divide
And slide. Once he looked back
At her who smiled so mindlessly; and wide
The whitening track behind her smiled until
It too closed over. Far away in her
He heard the roar of a hundred shunned shores
Rising like hope; his seed the thunder-wash
And swish of shingle, slow relinquished; store
On store of aggravation; with wave on wave
Of following wish—foamed over with love—
Combing him home.

Earth opened her knees and showed
A lip and lap of luxury
And many a slip between. On all sides
The tall cliffs rose like sighs; and far below,
Grotesticled and still, like long-ago-ness,
The cold sea wrinkled languidly and
Wrangled roundly in its orchid coils.
Still through all these eel-and-alley-ways of water
The wakeful bull wove on to where the lost wave
Wept and slept away to land.

Light as the last leaf-thin wave that laves
And chins the urchin-shell ashore and leaves

A bib of bubble-lace upon the sand,
So belly-landed, and so light, Europa.
She, O so full of herself, laughed and ran
Before the prancing bull who danced his hooves
Of dazzling drizzle after. And danced too
All the sand tassels of his ecstasy,
Nodding him on. Still he followed
And still she fled—calling, calling, calling
Across the upland lawns, along the fields
Cuckooing in the wood—a forward voice
And backward shadow drawing him on
Through all the lifting veils and darkening falls
Of his desire. For always as he looked
She leaked away. At his eyes' widest note
She narrowed into nothing. As he sued
She ceased. Softly he delved
Into her nest of selves and drew one out,
But O the rest were gone, and this
Was airy nothing and a stone. Quicker
Against the wall of sense he beat his ball
Of wits: quick as it went it came back quick
And soft as soft. What mirror-wall was this
That fed him to himself, that led
Him roundabout to his still-staring start?
Again the cry? Again the resonance!

Once, silent in water, as in a glass
He saw her pass, and darted forward; then,
Like a dare-laden dart that loses heart
And sides with air, he swerved and stood, swithering;
And still the arrow shivered where it struck.
The cheeks of air were burning where she passed.
O, there was never the like of her: a look,
And all the larks' tongues went laddering up
The spine of his sky, and the garrulous rooks
Of his gusto rose and spun on arias
Of air, and out of his plucked heart-string.

The pigeon-beat sprang pizzicato. Cheat
She was to leave him; fish that flash and leave
A false and staring face of studied emptiness
Were not more cold. And weak as water he
To waver so, who should be stone. Useless
This jelly-edge of adulation. Had he
No cold to harden him? Long
He stood there, dry, withdrawn as weed,
Gazing at his dismissal.
(Weed, after sea has gone, longs after it
Asks for it, is wistful.) That way she drew
Out of every eager tongue and feed of him.
How he leeched after her!
He longed to stop this longing, to burst
The thong, to be beholden to no one,
To wander at will, to squelch and to squander
Without regard, to fray off silently
Like children from their chiding; to be
Vapour and vagabond.
O to drone on in onlyness like the bee,
To stop and helicopter over the rose,
Or like a bird—that bit of looking-glass—
See all and take-in nothing, be mirror
And no more. But every hole said 'Have a heart!',
And every hill cried 'Hold!' Somewhere must greed
And godhead in him meet and mate.
Animal-man, god-man, the two must have
Her for hyphen and for life.

But no remembering air remarked her presence.
Only the hawk dangled its dark tidings
Overhead, and a shadow of silence
Fell. This land was death; webs of breath
On every bush; loneliness curled in the leaf;
The leech was king.
The shot bird hung in air, the blown rose
Forgot to fall.

Now hill-hurrying, now dale-dallying,
He stammered on in shining stealth among
The thieving glooms and tunnelled sidings
Of the wood. Thorns, those tear-alongs of gloom,
Extorted care from him. A backsprung branch
Of laughter lashed his face. And once
A whine of light went past. He winced. What hand
Had squeezed the whistle-bag of sloth, and shot
That shining quick at him? What fist
Had tightened? If only he could find it,
Prise it open, surprise it. If only
Each leaf here were a word, and every curse were a tree,
He would cover the world with his umbrage.
Rage jagged him. How he longed, quivered
To cudgel these rocks to jelly, to card
These reaches to grass. So, for miles and miles,
Resentment smelled and smouldered; though sometimes
Smoke broke into a glow, a smile. Sometimes, too,
Into his nostrils' violet caves he drew
A few saved scents of her, savouring them;
The green yet sweet; the purple O but bitter.
Often in eye-bright openings he passed
Heifers that half in love, and half in fright,
Tingled and lifted all their tails for flight.
But lightly along the railing of their looks
He drew his stare; and O what a hiccupping belly
Of bullying light went before him; how
He creamed his way through their gloom, leaving a wake
And wash of widening silence. Yet still
Their lowing slowed him as water sleeves
And slows. Once he stopped
To wonder and to widen at the sight
Of willowy birds that, sail-like, wiled their way
Between the winds. Birds show the shape of air;
As these words share the birds' shape, converting
Back again to air their spirit. Like stone
He stood there, his feet grown into roots

64

Of deep reluctance; quiet as the lake
Whose roofless and unruffled eye took in
The sky, as truth takes in a lie. Strange
How wildness weans the sense, withdraws the sight
From set response, feathers and furthers it.
All the wide air now crowded and keyholed
Through him. Cloud and clod were both more clear,
More particular; silence too was ear-lighted;
Scent was tented. He noticed the wren's nest,
Voluminously loved; the bee's furred foot,
The honeysuckle's hinge. A bead of blood
On a bird's beak told him the rose was sore
Today. The harsh grass was on edge last night
The blunt wind said. Deep in their cups he saw
The acorns sleep: and the hare—that leaping pulse—
Twitched past like water. He noticed, then,
A severed ear of iris borne away
On the reticent river: had *she* so feared
Its eavesdropping? Dared she pluck it? A peacock eye
Blinked beneath a stone. Had she thrown it there
From spite? Again that momentary cry!
Again she mushroomed into dumbness!
Ah, how could she expand out of his scope?
Sometimes it seemed as if a hush of hands
Blew everywhere like smoke, herding her on
And hoarding her. It was a day for hush,
Anyway. Even the loose leaves
That hung about in tatters of light talk,
Let fall their chattering latches at his shadow:
And the stuttering blackbird skittered away
Into the ditches, dropping its stitches:
And soft and seldom came the cry now, yet still
Through the bled air of her most pointed strike
He followed—like a haft and aftermath—
Europa. Through the suck and clap, pith and spit
Of sounding clay pounded the sulky bull,
Till suddenly his path flared to a fan.

Here was harder ground, great scoop and scope. At each clop
Of his chiselled hooves the stones came to heel,
And fiery spirts of grass flew from his toes.
How *she* had silked and sleeked these grasses flat
As any sickle in her passing: and still
The galleried leaves and grieving doves longed
And looked after her. Cautiously he looked
In every grove for her. O frugal love!
Cuckoo folly! For he was the light leaf,
And she the shadow under; half-lift it
And she flees delinquently
Like water every way gone wild,
Water, the stone's child.

Midway they met
Where daylight and delight broke through the roof.
There in a tambourine clearing of shaking leaves,
Where nightly the ambient moth on its undulate thong
Of nothingness dances, she flashed;
She at the touch of whose name
All his tongue's tapers would flame.
O what wonders can happen in woods
Or in words, what two may touch, what gloom
Can ignite, halves hyphenate; what dead ends
And ands join answering hands.
As when the rounding sounding bee at last
Alights and kisses the sill of its stillness,
Its singing skein at length wound into a ball,
So all his dreamy wanderings had come
To one true pass; here through the gate of horn
They threaded to be born. Why should she shir
And shudder then? Scared by his lashing air
She curled back into gloom,
The silent pleas of her eyes
Jumping from place to place
Of his bold unblinking stare. Cold, he thought,
Cold as cut-glass

That holds a burning eye of candle-light
Her body is. Its beauty's to distract
The tender lover, its answer's to deflect
His anxious longing and to make it linger
In thinking ways; it fractures and delays
His single gaze. That hovering face,
That cold shoulder and the swelling hopes
Below, have no warm arm or base
To widen or embrace one.
But stiff, as if in alarm,
She bristles into beauty. O a thousand thistles
Of glass and kisses of ice she is.
Fire in a thousand mirrors is the eye
That looks at her with warmth; and each light facet shows
Only a dancing midge, a jigging image
Of changing joy. Gently on the swell
Of her he rose and fell, reflectively.
Then as between two lifts the candle-flame
Sinks to rise stiff, tip-toe, and finger-still,
Stretching at length to its ecstatic aim
As if from slackness it had drawn its fill,
So on knees of night the bull sank
Lowly to his socket,
And so—all stitches stretched—on toes of light
The god rose slowly. How could she not,
Hooked-up to that hawkpoint of hovering love,
Feel fear? Seeing him assume
That luminous image, did she divine
The blind millenium of mind behind
The upstart moment, the deep duplicity
Of flesh and spirit, clod and cloud, the make-and-break
Of clamouring animal and calm god,
And man the amalgam?
Ah but she had neither ear nor air
For argument, who now could only stare,
Round, thoughtless, oughtless, at the shapeless god,
Who slowly rose before her.

In tiers and terraces went clambering up,
Out of his huff of hooves, his blazing cape
And carapace of darkness, covering all
The clinging undertow of dearth like hope.
And in that darkness wrestled the lone god,
Jolted in every joint like elbowing flame
That strove for overthrow. What here had grasp
Of anything? What smoke-scream called him forth
So suddenly? She saw his osier-arms
Sprout, his fisted hooves fray into finger-fronds,
The abrupt bull-neck extenuate. A shin
Inched up to knee and sunshined into thigh.
Back into lack the entrances all led,
But all the vents evoked the forward god
Who rose and faced Europa.

O how the blush belled in her body now,
And how the confused water of her wits
Began to cloud and boil.
He from her confusion took delight,
She from his joy took more confusion still,
And still the dizzy circle swirled them in
And swung them up in swings of argument
And roundabout agreement. Each way they swayed
And swirled alternately, were two and one
By turns, opposed and yet appeased:
And, in between, the pulsing spirit flowed
In threads of love; love, the silver thread
Of thirst in every well, the saving vein
Of soil in every soul. Knee-deep in grass
The god knelt then and hooped his patient hands
Over her frog-like body's fluttering vein
As if to capture it. Ah but to have
Was not to hold. Swallows that sleet and slight
The airy eaves in flight were not more light
Than he at play. And yet
A blindman's praises of haze

Were not so lacking in phrase
As night-light fingers were that wary day
Wanting in subtlety.
Anomaly of love that less-than-light
And almost-lost should most molest and tease
The nettled flesh. O how the greedy gaps
Of rapture in her ran to feed
On deprivation, eagerly gulping up
Each sharp repulse. Gaps are not empty.
Those who, living in gloom, employ all lights
To plume and amplify it, best know
That blackness is not lack; more lives in it
Than meets the eye. Ice has fire-crackle in it,
Heat has frosts to free it from its laxity.
Tethered to each other's throats,
Skinny saint and roguish satyr
Strangle on one string like goats.
O fructifying friction, furthering both!
Sharpness is all. Defection or devotion,
Each fears and foreskins each, and whets the edge
For issue. Look how in this one man
The animal ran on, the god drew back
From brute rapacity, reining and rearing,
Yet the tormenting rub and rob between
Was itch and ecstasy to him.
That curling wool of mist
That bore Europa first and all her chatter
Of girls, grew where two instincts kissed and kicked
In lag of ice, alacrity of water.
O rise and fall of breath, ins and outs
Of a season—all's fanned by vacillation.
He was but tumbling timber in her waves,
And in her sea's accordeon-squeeze and swell
He rose and fell now. Tides bore him back
Surprised. An undertow of hope
Returned him. Each lag increased his longing.
What passionate rhythm in the blood had hinged

This shingle-flesh, swung him between
The dying depth of birth, the deepening sea
Of death? What flux of generation bore him on
To this one woman, flung him in this shore?

Here on the sill
Of silence and assent
She waited wordless, though her body spoke.
As trundling thunders pause
And pitch their lightning tents upon the hush,
Or as the darkling bird
Crowds all its longings into one last rush, so
Her backward breasts like trumped-up charges rose
And brazened out his coming. Three times
Three times the dust thrilled and throbbed
And rills of answer ran between the stones.
Three times the rod gulped and pulsed
Like shaken rope.
And louder drummed the blood-light in his ears,
Stiffer the lift, rounder the hour at last
That struck for home. Love, like a lick of oil,
That softly clicks the lock and often,
Slid over her then and loosed her backward wards
To one sprung cry—'Zeus!' O the fountain-throw!
The twitching hitch! the quiet!

Go, sun and moon! Come, musk and cinnamon,
Assume me now;
Sing me the dying god, the night's denial and
The light-cock-crow.
Let all the mournful musics flow
Over his morning deeps, and mask
The blind bull bellowing slow, the sea-bell
Tolling low in funeral-gloom.
Light fails within the wood.
The last, the best pieces of brightness fall
Into the base grasses that appropriate all.

O, as grass amasses grass,
May sleep after sleep, loved over by leaves,
Engross those two, house them and hush them
In arms of amaranth,
And may the nodding moth of myth
In every mouth take breath and wing now,
And dance these words out in honour of that wedding.

PAN AND SYRINX

Across the heavy sands running they came,
She like his shadow shot on before him,
But bit by bit it shortened to full stop
And noonday dot. Then, just within his gasp
She faded, in the sunburst of his joy
Expunged. He had not time to countermand
His smirk of pride, or blandly to run on
As if the running were his only ploy
And she a by-play. Stupidly he stood
Looking in every flaw of air for her,
And staring close at every bird that rose
Out of the reeds, his shock eyes jumping on
From place to place of her nonentity.
Where had she gone, the hussy? Had she flown
Clean out of time and space? A dream? But no,
For still her nestlings' beaks gaped after her,
And still his nostrils quivered and fanned wide
Like twanged elastic in an ecstasy;
Ear and eye still gonged her striking image.

He called her loudly, then: 'Syrinx! Syrinx!'
But nothing blinked: the ignorant ox browsed on,
And the reflective river brassily
Slewed by without a pause. At his foot
Out of the bearded iris rose the bee
In drizzling sibilance. But angrily
Pan stood, and stamped the sudden edge, his hands
Chawed savagely at the sedge. But what, what
Was this they held so closely choked? A reed?
Was ever reed like this one, coolest green,
And blue as if the ice-roots ran in it?
He opened his hands, and looked. O now he knew
The subterfuge of flesh. So this was how
She gave the slip to his lubricity.
He broke into a goat, the Spirit gone:
The Spirit flown, *she* split into a reed:
Green reed, red animal were complements,

72

And neither could the other venerate.
Her he could feel, but never enter now:
Him she could enter, but could never feel:
So red and green must wrangle endlessly.
Ah, why had he come here? Was it to see
Grass shaken by the wind? Would nothing ease
The nettle-tease of flesh, the salted taws
Of lust?

Grief crowded in his eyes and looked at her,
Till, fogged by too-long thought, he turned away
Lugubriously, lugging the bruised reed:
And with no backward look he went
With bold subtracting steps across the plain
And vanished in the upland groves and haze.
And afterwards was heard
His starving flute crying in stony places,
Calling for love, for love the heavenly rain,
To fall and make his green reed nymph again.
And still he cried 'Syrinx', and still he drew
Her only answer from the reed he blew.

STORMY NIGHT

Is this the street? Never a sign of life,
The swinging lamp throws everything about;
But see! from that sly doorway, like a knife
The gilt edge of inviting light slides out
And in again—the very sign
Of her whose slightest nod I lately thought was mine;

But not now.
Knock! and the night-flowering lady
Opens, and across the brilliant sill
Sees me standing there so dark and shady
Hugging the silences of my ill-will;
Wildly she turns from me—But no, my love,
This foot's within the door, this hand's without the glove.

Well may you tremble now, and say there was nothing meant,
And curl away from my care with a 'Please, my dear!',
For though you were smoke, sucked up by a raging vent,
I'd follow you through every flue of your fear,
And over your faraway arms I'll mountain and cone
In a pillar of carolling fire and fountaining stone.

O strike the gong of your wrong, raise the roof of your rage,
Fist and foist me off with a cloud of cries,
What do I care for all your footling rampage?
On your light-in-gale blows my larking caresses will rise,
But—Why so still? What! are you weeping, my sweet?
Ah heart, heart, look! I throw myself at your feet.

LENT

Mary Magdalene, that easy woman,
Saw, from the shore, the seas
Beat against the hard stone of Lent,
Crying, 'Weep, seas, weep
For yourselves that cannot dent me more.

O more than all these, more crabbed than all stones,
And cold, make me, who once
Could leap like water, Lord. Take me
As one who owes
Nothing to what she was. Ah, naked.

My waves of scent, my petticoats of foam
Put from me and rebut;
Disown. And that salt lust stave off
That slavered me—O
Let it whiten in grief against the stones

And outer reefs of me. Utterly doff,
Nor leave the lightest veil
Of feeling to heave or soften.
Nothing cares this heart
What hardness crates it now or coffins.

Over the balconies of these curved breasts
I'll no more peep to see
The light procession of my loves
Surf-riding in to me
Who now have eyes and alcove, Lord, for Thee.'

'Room, Mary', said He, 'ah make room for me
Who am come so cold now
To my tomb.' So, on Good Friday,
Under a frosty moon
They carried Him and laid Him in her womb.

A grave and icy mask her heart wore twice,
But on the third day it thawed,
And only a stone's-flow away
Mary saw her God.
Did you hear me? Mary saw her God!

Dance, Mary Magdalene, dance, dance and sing,
For unto you is born
This day a King. 'Lady', said He,
'To you who relent
I bring back the petticoat and the bottle of scent.'

THE SWAN

Bottomed by tugging combs of water
The slow and loath swan slews and looks
Coldly down through chutes of stilled chatter
Upon the shadows in flight among the stones.

Into abashed confusions of ooze
It dips, and from the muddy fume
The silver and flute-like fishes rise
Endlessly up through all their octaves of gloom

To where the roofed swan suavely swings
Without qualm on the quivering wave
That laves it on, with elbowing wings held wide
Under its eyes' hugged look and architrave.

Jonquil-long its neck adjudicates
Its body's course; aloof and cool
It cons the nonchalant and unseeing air
With its incurious and dispassionate stare.

Slow, slow, it slides, as if not to chafe
The even sleeve of its approach
Stretched stiff and oval in front of it,
Siphoning it on, selfless, silent, and safe.

On that grey lake, frilled round with scufflings
Of foam and milled with muttering
I saw lingering, late and lightless,
A single swan, swinging, sleek as a sequin.

Negligently bright, wide wings pinned back,
It mooned on the moving water,
And not all the close and gartering dark
Or gathering wind could lift or flatter
That small and dimming image into flight;
Far from shore and free from foresight,
Coiled in its own indifferent mood
It held the heavens, shores, waters and all their brood.

THE AIRMAN

Afterwards he may take thought
And praise, who now may not
Move farther than the moment's jot,
Afterwards who lives may dare
To stop and spit and backward stare
Up at the proved and friendly air.
But not now, no, not now: who knows
Which moment falls the forward rose?
What hole may open at the feet
Of him who boasts himself complete?
Or whose the mercy, whose the might
Sustains the tight-rope of his flight?
His armour's to be unespied,
Therefore he strips off all his pride,
Assumes the cerements of air
That has no here, and owns no there.
Then should death meet him it will see
Nothing but clear neutrality,
And, gazing still, its eyes will pass
Purely through him as if through glass.
And yet, compulsive and complete
His fate caves darkly at his feet;
Far in the bottoms of the world
His path is smoothed, his pit is curled.
O long the flight but short the spill
That lands the cock on his dunghill.
Balanced on searchlight-tip his plane
May glint like tinsel, fall like rain:
Wadded in fluffy salvoes he
May see the silent blood flow free:
And look! out of the blue unrolls
His vapoury bandage, scrolls on scrolls
Of lightest linen following fast
As if to fold and overcast.
Then praise not now his skill or nerve
Who knows how errors made him swerve
From his dead reckonings that must

Have milled and ground him into dust.
He knows the smooth handrail of flight
Has stuttering verticals of fright;
Lives by death's negligence and not
By any guards the gods allot.
To meet with all but go with none
That is his fate whose single fun
And only ease is to be found
Upon the bosom of the round
And randy air: to it he'll give
Up everything that he may live.
Then keep your praise, nor ask him why
He pierces you with pin-sight eye;
Nor smile compliantly when he
Fobs-off applause, for yours may be
The grin that will precipitate
The gravelly avalanche of fate.
Gravely each night he raises hell,
And he has seen great Gabriel
Jog God's elbow, bid Him look
Up from his absorbing Book
To—absentmindedly—admire
The rhododendron banks of fire
Flowering from roots that upward point
Their pleading hands, all out-of-joint,
Till God, replete with sacrifice,
Rubs planes like motes out of His eyes.

Afterwards he may take thought
And praise, who now may not
Move farther than the moment's jot.
Meanwhile within the mindless deep
Of his humility he'll keep
A waking seed of self that will
One day dance on every hill.
These are dead men; like seed they fly
Widely on every wind, and die

Into their pride that there may grow
More humility below:
Not till that tuberous trumpet breaks the clay
Will they rise up, their resurrection day.

THE FALL

O angel of the ledges of our dread
On whose jellied edges each joy is dandled
Gently, like danger—now, like daws on trees
Unbalancing, turn our dread into ease
And let the fall open our wings' eyes wide
In wonder at ourselves who were so slow
To float out on the rootless raft of air
With flowing hold.
The Fall! the fall, from that safe tree
Of love we so much feared to leave, elates
And lifts our other selves to life. Only
By daring do we learn our manyness.
Safety stints us, turns us to stone, to one.
This always-gibbering between fear and hope
Doubles our life, and is the bloody pulse
Of every vein. O angel of our dread,
Delicately cater for us rough feeders
Who ask a stone; and duly give us bread.

CHRIST WALKING ON THE WATER

Slowly, O so slowly, longing rose up
In the forenoon of his face, till only
A ringlet of fog lingered round his loins.
And fast he went down beaches all weeping
With weed, and waded out. Twelve tall waves,
Sequent and equated, hollowed and followed.
O what a cock-eyed sea he walked on,
What poke-ends of foam, what elbowings
And lugubrious looks, what ebullient
And contumacious musics. Always there were
Hills and holes, pills and poles, a wavy wall
And bucking ribbon caterpillaring past
With glossy ease. And often, as he walked,
The slow curtains of swell swung open and showed,
Miles and smiles away, the bottle-boat
Flung on a wavering frond of froth that fell
Knee-deep and heaved thigh-high. In his forward face
No cave of afterthought opened; to his ear
No bottom clamour climbed up; nothing blinked.
For he was the horizon, he the hub,
Both bone and flesh, finger and ring of all
This clangourous sea. Docile, at his toe's touch
Each tottering dot stood roundaboutly calm
And jammed the following others fast as stone.
The ironical wave smoothed itself out
To meet him, and the mocking hollow
Hooped its back for his feet. A spine of light
Sniggered on the knobbly water, ahead.
But he like a lover, caught up,
Pushed past all wrigglings and remonstrances
And entered the rolling belly of the boat
That shuddered and lay still. And he lay there
Emptied of his errand, oozing still. Slowly
The misted mirror of his eyes grew clear
And cold, the bell of blood tolled lower,
And bright before his sight the ocean bared
And rolled its horrible bold eye-balls endlessly

In round rebuke. Looking over the edge
He shivered. Was this the way he had come?
Was that the one who came? The whole wieldy world
And all the welded welt that he had walked on
Burst like a plate into purposelessness.
All, all was gone, the fervour and the froth
Of confidence, and flat as water was
The sad and glassy round. Somewhere, then,
A tiny flute wriggled like a worm, O so lonely.
A ring of birds rose up and wound away
Into nothingness. Beyond himself he saw
The settled steeples, and breathing beaches
Running with people. But he,
He was custodian to nothing now,
And boneless as an empty sleeve hung down.
Down from crowned noon to cambered evening
He fell, fell, from white to amber, till night
Slid over him like an eyelid. And he,
His knees drawn up, his head dropped deep,
Curled like a question mark asleep.

THE NET

Quick, woman, in your net
Catch the silver I fling!
O I am deep in your debt,
Draw tight, skin-tight, the string,
And rake the silver in.
No fisher ever yet
Drew such a cunning ring.

Ah, shifty as the fin
Of any fish this flesh
That, shaken to the shin,
Now shoals into your mesh,
Bursting to be held in;
Purse-proud and pebble-hard,
Its pence like shingle showered.

Open the haul, and shake
The fill of shillings free,
Let all the satchels break
And leap about the knee
In shoals of ecstasy.
Guineas and gills will flake
At each gull-plunge of me.

Though all the Angels, and
Saint Michael at their head,
Nightly contrive to stand
On guard about your bed,
Yet none dare take a hand,
But each can only spread
His eagle-eye instead.

But I, being man, can kiss
And bed-spread-eagle too;
All flesh shall come to this,
Being less than angel is,
Yet higher far in bliss
As it entwines with you.

Come, make no sound, my sweet;
Turn down the candid lamp
And draw the equal quilt
Over our naked guilt.

SPRING-DANCE

Late, late. But lift now the diffident fiddle and fill
The dancing bed with light and the bud-room with thunder
Till all the floors fall in and walls laugh under
The envious knockings of neighbours, and over the sill
The daffodil day looks in. You who are standing,
Yes you—kick up your kilt of legs like a gawky foal
And fling away there! On every leaf-landing
The lovers are forking, on every stair-air
They are larking: the dog-days are barking
In all the backyards. So off with your careful sark
And lift the diffident fiddle. O the lilt's not difficult, if
You have soil in your soul. God in the clod, then, begin
And cloud into powder your foot and fetlock of clay
As you clout the floor and claw your next-of-skin
In a fug of guffaws. Ah, there's never a fog
That fails to ivy and over the wall of its huff
And hangover. Not even a gruff one who won't
Give a heave—and a fig for all leaves!—and have after,
(How the daft words proliferate in me like laughter!)
As Jack after Jill. So off with your careful sark and lift
The diffident fiddle. Can no one cajole you
To hyphenate hands in the dance, and piece out its pauses
With passes? Listen! The night-cocks are throwing their crowing
Far beyond sight of their own height and knowing
Into the light. You, only, are lacking
The jocular glow. Look how the gales brag and bring
Surprises of birds all paradised-over by Spring.

CAROL

Deep in the fading leaves of night
There lay the flower that darkness knows,
Till winter stripped and brought to light
The most incomparable Rose
That blows, that blows.

The flashing mirrors of the snow
Keep turning and returning still:
To see the lovely child below
And hold him is their only will;
Keep still, keep still.

And to let go his very cry
The clinging echoes are so slow
That still his wail they multiply
Though he lie singing now below,
So low, so low.

Even the doves forget to grieve
And gravely to his greeting fly
And the lone places that they leave
All follow and are standing by
On high, on high.

SONG

Lord, if I had a lathe
To turn out words as fine
And fit as any turd
That ever fell behind:
If I could swathe after swathe
Of swithering dancing ears
Lay stiff in listening line
Behind the advancing shears:
Then swift as any bird
I'd fill the volute of your ear
With one flute-note so loud, so clear,
That never after could you bear
A sound less apt, less debonair,
For in your mould of mind its wet
And molten ore would wind and set.

EVENING

The shadows ladder out. And lance-like
Over the slow reluctant gold-glue river
The dragonfly's gonfalon, like a shout,
Glances blue through the shiver
And fidget of midges that flag the flow
Far below. Look! what jag did it fling
As it stopped? what jibe deliver
As it stared there entranced? Yet at once
Its daring's forgot. In a flash if goes off,
In a sliver. O it cares not a thing. Air
Is its only knowing, its foe and forgiver.

THE TRAIN

There with a screech stuck in her hair like a feather
She strikes through signals, sequels, stares, and significations
With equal squeal; scattering the stuck tons of thunder
In tunnels like tins staccato; alliterating
The laddering lights and escalatoring clatter till
At last she assonants free. The elbowing air
Ushers her on, cushions and repercussions her
In its indulgent hush. And always her weeping past
Wallabies wildly away in smokes and hang-
Overs of gloom across the long-ago fields that once were mine.
Long ago? No. The cataract still hangs
In tatters as it did. On the same thong of air
The hawk impends. Still leans the lonely tree
Above the only lake, its ageing shade
Unwrinkled in the shaking glass. And still
The fountain eyelashes a stony stare.
All's as I left it, place and pose and weather
That once was willed for ever. Once again
I look out from the train,
I see the solemn child, and wave to it in vain.

ARMAGH

There is a through-otherness about Armagh
Of tower and steeple,
Up on the hill are the arguing graves of the kings,
And below are the people.

Through-other as the rooks that swoop and swop
Over the sober hill
Go the people gallivanting from shop to shop
Guffawing their fill.
And the little houses run through the market-town
Slap up against the great,
Like the farmers all clabber and muck walking arm by arm
With the men of estate.

Raised at a time when Reason was all the rage,
Of grey and equal stone,
This bland face of Armagh covers an age
Of clay and feather and bone.

Through-other is its history, of Celt and Dane,
Norman and Saxon,
Who ruled the place and sounded the gamut of fame
From cow-horn to klaxon.

There is a through-otherness about Armagh
Delightful to me,
Up on the hill are the graves of the garrulous kings
Who at last can agree.

THE TRINITY

Down the darkened hall of brain
Darts the tiny mouse of pain,
Quick as thought the waking cat
Of consciousness scoots from the mat,

Elastically catches it,
Statically lets it go
Slack again, but snatches it
Lightly back on its yo-yo.

Till in the vast and breathing hall
A thousand sleepers wake and call
'Curse the cat and curse the mouse,
—And curse, God curse, this bloody house.'

God who did send this I to cry
Between two selves on Calvary,
God who in darkness all forlorn
Between two thieving moods was torn,

(The nagging cat of thought, the mouse
Of niggling guilt that runs this house)
Make these two malefactors one
Within this I
That soon must die,
And then will rise the Sun, the Sun,
The trinity, the three-in-one.

THE HARVEST FIELD

There is nothing to note; only the mowers
Moving like doom. Slowly, one by one,
A gloom of bees rises and soon snores
Thunder-headed away into the sun.

Listen! Listen! do you hear the hiss
Of the scythe in the long grasses
That are silently tingling like bells that kiss
And repel as the wind passes.

There in the last care and core of corn
The hare is couched: not till the mowers flash
Their smiling scythes, and all its walls are shorn
Will the wild creature dash
Into the wintry air of hound and horn.

Listen! Listen! do you hear the hiss
Of the scythe in the long grasses of your laughter?
More is mowed than you know, for this
Is Time's swathe, and you are the one that he's after.

APOLLO AND DAPHNE

Look how her close defences laddered now
In one lean stroke, flawed and flowed like water
Zipping open a Zuyder Zee
Of privacy. What does it matter
If she lay passive and refused to strike?

For when the flying hare, her breast mud-beaten,
Hears the hounds gain and give tongue greedily
A field away, and feels their huddled thud
Thundering and darkening the ground before her,
How her breath leaves her, and her feet connive,
And hungry eyes let go their hold of home,
And all her heart is lifted up from her,
No longer arguing, agreeing now
With her devoted and devouring fate;
And, floating out upon the wind, her cry
Circles the scene with careless quisling eye.

So this doomed woman, hounded and brought low,
Wheels round and meets her captor toe to toe
And face to face. Deep in the other's eyes
She sees herself, and smiles, a solemn mime
There in the mirror where her halves embrace
And consummate the marriage of the chase.

For from that last tip-toppling tower of Time
Lifted above herself her heart can see
The self that followed and the self that fled
(through all the long and round about of days)
Closing the circle irremediably
Of life and death, in one brief binding gaze:
And in the awful night of pain long-drawn
Rises a conflagration of peace, a bloody dawn.

RESURRECTION

AN EASTER SEQUENCE

'*O vos omnes,*
Qui transitis per viam, et videte,
Si est dolor similis sicut dolor meus,
Attendite universi populi, et videte
dolorem meum, dolorem meum.'

*Tell ye the daughter of Sion, Behold thy King cometh unto
thee . . .*

It was a deliberate moment, and O
Just in the nick and nook of time he came,
The timeless One, to reclaim us. Everything waited,
Everything peaked and pointed to his coming.
The morning rose up early, a tip toe of a day,
All was light and elastic, the birds chirping away,
The air chipped into buds. People were on their knees
With wonder, and some were weeping. And when at last He
    appeared
—The Hero—such a hail of huzzas and hosannahs as sprang up!
Why, the very house-tops rose to the occasion and broke
Their hush and hung out all their hearts' hoorays.
This was glory. Yet, he knew the swings of men, and now
It was the old story.
The day too bright to last, the crowd too loud to stay.
Those who magnified now would mock Him tomorrow,
Those who deified, defy. Already He saw
The shadow of Doubt, the pickpocket of conviction,
Move through the crowd. And far away and behind
Their fume and furore of glory he heard the door
Of doom slam; meanwhile all was gay
And like a King he came triumphant up this way.

And when He was come into Jerusalem, all the city was moved,
saying, Who is this?

O it was no day at all for doubt or for cloud,
The children ran cheering in front, the birds sang loud,
The very trees were bowed; and the butterfly leaves
Took off to greet him.
But he rode loftily by as if uninvolved in the glory,
And the ass, as if understanding the story,
Carried him sadly on to a tame
And lamentable conclusion.
To meet with all and go with none
That was his doom who mediates and makes one
The split that was in man since time began.
But how to heal the breach? how to reach across?
Ay, that was the only answer now—the Cross!
Deep in his mind the roots ran that way, and his fate
Was fixed. The tree was grown that stood on Calvary,
What was to do was done. Still, it was a glad day.
Let the bells all ring, let them have their fling,
For this way led to glory and to everlasting Spring.

Now when the even was come, he sat down with the twelve.

Twelve heads hugged in a ring
Twelve hands breaking bread
Twelve hearts bursting to sing
The song of life from the dead.

Now the moment had come; he must love them and leave them
Yet without losing; this is the mystery of losing.
In the world, of course, it is different; there, every love of life
Of person, place, or thing, is a boon and a beauty
That comes in the morning so freely. Yet, in the afternoon,
Fearful of losing it we freeze it into a duty
And judge it our due. And then what surprise
When in the evening it dies.
O if only we had faith enough not to confine
And coffin the thing that we love, faith enough to receive
It just when it came, insight enough to let go and believe
That each morning would bring it again,
We would not have to grieve over the thing that was slain.
So he spoke to them at supper, so he figured it forth
In the breaking of bread
To those who were his twelve selves, dear as his own soul.
For all these selves his soul had for sieves
To let fall his story
As snow falls in flakes; yet who knows if it gives
One half of what it knows of the whole glory.

And as they did eat, he said, Verily I say unto you, that one of you shall betray me.

Name him not, Name him not, nor constellate
The one who led him to his fate. Nevertheless
Judas was part of Jesus.
For the god has always a foot of clay, and the soul
Grows in soil, the flower has a dark root.
And deep in all is the base collaborator.
The betrayer is ever oneself, never another.
All must say, 'Lord is it I?' There is always
Evil in Goodness, lust in love, dust on the dove's foot,
And without it purity's groundless. And the Cross
Had never been.

Then cometh Jesus with them unto a place called Gethsemane.

It was a lovely night,
A night for weddings and for water.
Going out into the cold glow he felt washed
And clean of people. The garden had an air
Of waiting about it, as if the leaves were bent
On eavesdropping. And the rain
Scented the air with more-than-midnight pain
And the wet trees that had nowhere to go
Stood round and gazed at the One walking there below
In agony. Ebb and flow, to and fro, Yes and No;
Doubt assailed him. Which and what to do? This much must be
    admitted,
We live between two worlds, faith and doubt,
Like breath. The air that one breathes does not care
Whether it's in or out; it's not in love with life
Or death. And yet we do not dare to hold it long,
But must let go to find again. So with faith,
With love, with everything. Now at the cross-roads,
Middled and muddled he stood.
This was it. And it was night. 'Nevertheless Thy will be done.'
That thought made morning of it, gave him ease, and issue.
He knew now how to stay and stare it out
And already the torches approached the garden.

Now Peter sat without in the Palace.

Tenebrae now; and quenched as if by doubt
One after one the torches all go out
In token of the twelve who went away
Each after other on the fatal day.
That fateful night,
Late in the palace, something strange occurred.
A spider lit on his hand, and he threw it away
But it returned to his hand on a thread;
He threw it away again, and again away,
And again till his fingers were dripping
And webbed with threads, but, horrible! still it came back
Like a truth that could not be denied,
The truth he had three times denied;
Peter desisted. He listened. In the cold dawn
The cock was throwing aloft its threefold crown
And aureole of sound. Then he remembered
The meaning.
In the dark blue and petering hour
Of night it sang, and looking out,
He saw the tree dance into flower
Enlisting all the morning's light;
It was the bloody Judas tree,
And on it hung not him, but *me.*

Whether of the twain will ye that I release unto you? They said,
Barabbas.

We will always beg the question.
Jesus did not belong to this time;
Their clocks all said he came before his chime,
All the lamps of the city declared him a stranger,
A nobody come out of darkness, and therefore a danger
To law and to order. Must it always be so?
Must we always make light of the devil we know
And dark of the god who is ranger? O
It is easy to choose what's dead right, right
—So we say—to refuse to live wrong; so we move
In thick circles of self, and the lean dog-rose
Looks for the hole in our hedge and lurks
In our thorn waiting to leap out of lack
Into bloom like the god in the manger.

And when he had scourged Jesus, he delivered him to be
crucified.

The took him out to die.
The lark was shaking out its acres of song in the sky
And the sun shone. People looked up and remarked
What a wonderful day it was going to be
And the cheering boys ran on in front of the crowd,
And the cheeky ones waited to stare.
                                          Once he noticed
A blind man whom he had healed looking at him
With horrified eyes as much as to say
'Was it for this I was given sight by the god that day?'
He turned away. If only this had been an important death,
If only he knew that the people who barracked him now
Had been travelling years and years to reach this place.
But they were casual passers-by and their interest was jaded.
Yet it was all as he had expected, and
He would not avoid or evade it. Far away
A spool of birds was spinning above the hill,
And still Pilate sat in the empty court beneath,
Sucking threads of thoughtfulness through his teeth.

And they crucified him.

This was a rough death, there was nothing tidy about it,
No sweetness, nothing noble.
Everything stuck out awkwardly and angular:
The clumsy soldier brought the wrong basket of nails;
And the couriers—those sticky fly-papers of events—
Did not even bother to cover his sticky end,
Or carry it home to Rome. For them the war in Gaul
Was more important; the ship of state sailed on,
Leaving him bogging in the backward seas.
Still, that is how things always happen, lousily,
But later on, the heart edits them lovingly,
Abstracts the jeers and jags, imports a plan
Into the pain, and calls it history.
We always go back to gloss over some roughness,
To make the past happen properly as we want it to happen.
But this was a hard death. At the time
There was no room for thought.
How often he had hearsed and rehearsed this hour.
But when you come up against it all the good words about it
Are less than breath. It is hard to turn the other cheek
When both have been slapped:
                    Yes, it was a hard death.

Now there stood by the Cross of Jesus his mother . . .

A mist opened and closed its eyes before him,
And in it he saw her looking at him
The untouchable terrible god.
O what ladders of longing led up from her
To him, what steps and depths of memory ran down;
He remembered the happy days in Galilee
When he was heaven's hub; the heap of smoking grass,
The bubble-pipe, the light upon the wall,
The children in the far garden looking for the lost ball,
And Mary calling him. He was always so distant
In those lonely days. O if only
He had mattered less, she wondered, if only
She had mastered him more, would he then
Have been like other men, a flat satisfied plain?
But no. In him mountains of onlyness rose
Snow-high. Dayspring was in his eyes
At midnight. And he would not come down
From his far purpose even for her who was
The root that raised him to this Cross and crown
Of thorns. Yet tenderly he spoke
Goodbye now, his voice choking and dry.
And as she went away, leaving him to die,
The vast moon of his cry rose up upon the darkness.
His heart broke.

About the ninth hour Jesus cried with a loud voice, saying,
Eli, Eli, lama sabacthani?

His breath came in threads; his words were not his own.
He was dying now.
The sun refused to look, and the sky
Closed up its eye. Only the windows of his wounds.
Were wide open, and the red curtains of blood
Blew out into the storm, torn to ribbons.
He could no longer fend death off.
Slow, slow, loath to go, hope holds up its head
Though feet are so sawn through, like a sawn tree that stands
Long, then with one blinding run and blundering tear
Of last despair, scattering its brains and branches on the air
Slumps, lumps, pitches headlong and thuds, a log clodded
    clean.
So his last cry and acquiescence. And the vast wall
Of people drew back before that dying fall.
God was dead.

*And, behold, the vail of the temple was rent in twain from the top to
the bottom; and the earth did quake and the rocks rent;*

Now was the world's back broken; the darkness
Heaved in half, the wells rose up in walls
And fell in floods; and earth's own gorge
Rose and retched out its coffins. Everywhere
Lightnings lashed, and the curled thunder rolled
Its bolts over the crowd that broke and ran before its crash.
Each flash showed them in a different flight.
And in the downpour only the soldiers stood
Sodden and awed beneath the Cross. 'This was the son of God!'
To them the eliminating moment was
The illuminating one. Now all was still.
And on the desolate plain behind the hill
An ass brayed. Its palmy days were over.

*And there was Mary Magdalene and the other Mary, sitting over
against the sepulchre . . .*

It is always the women who are the Watchers
And keepers of life: they guard our exits
And our entrances. They are both tomb and womb,
End and beginning. Bitterly they bring forth
And bitterly take back the light they gave.
The last to leave and still the first to come,
They circle us like sleep or like the grave.
Earth is their element, and in it lies
The seed and silence of the lighted skies,
The seasons with their fall and slow uprise,
Man with his sight and militant surmise.
It is always the women who are the Watchers
And Wakeners.

In the end of the Sabbath, as it began to dawn towards the first day of the week, came Mary Magdalene.

The tomb, the tomb, that
Was her core and care, her one sore.
The light had hardly scarleted the dark
Or the first bird sung when Mary came in sight
With eager feet. Grief, like last night's frost,
Whitened her face and tightened all her tears.
It was there, then, there at the blinding turn
Of the bare future that she met her past.
She only heard this Angel tell her how
The holding stone broke open and gave birth
To her dear Lord, and how his shadow ran
To meet him like a dog.
And as the sun
Burns through the simmering muslins of the mist
Slowly his darkened voice, that seemed like doubt,
Morninged into noon; the summering bees
Mounted and boiled over in the bell-flowers.
'Come out of your jail, Mary', he said, 'the doors are open
And joy has its ears cocked for your coming.
Earth now is no place to mope in. So throw away
Your doubt, cast every clout of care,
Hang all your hallelujahs out
This airy day.'

* * *

SUMMER JOURNEY

Now it's July, hot and sleepy and still;
The noontide hanging motionless over the hill
Like a pike in a pool. And the glossy flies
Are flashing like great sun-whips across the eyes.
Summer is at its height,
The hastening season halted in its flight,
Its fans fixed.
And here we are in the Pays-Basque, travelling through Soule,
Labourd, and Basse-Navarre—names more musical to me
Than musk or kumiss or mangosteen.
Guéthary where the Atlantic curled in and cauliflowered up,
And the lightning jagged the sky like icicles:
Bidarry in the evening, the vines veining the hillside,
And the hills drawn up over our heads like shawls.
And us talking all night of war and Resistance.
Remember the Pyrenees, with their hundred double-chins,
Remember Soure, the sheep bells on the road,
And the panniered donkeys; the smuggler's path to Spain,
And the lovely inns; the meal at Mauléon;
The mayor's home-made liquor at Ustaritz
That Sunday afternoon. O
Remember the people so kind: remember the night you got blind
On Pernod?
And remember those great sleepy houses with their wide and
    wavy roofs
That cover cattle and people and wine and copper pans:
Houses eyelashed and shuttered against the summer heat,
Blindly white outside but with nests of darkness in them
As reticent and withdrawn as the Basques with their thin-pursed
    lips.
Slow country, rooted in resistance, not in rest.
Slow over the wall the fat peaches fall.
Slowly across the all-absorbing fields
Collusive move the peasant and his plough.
And slowly down the street the ox comes now
With winking bell. How it gives one the feel
Of the creaking cart and the ever-turning wheel.

Slow country, but quick people. What's so gay
As the little Basque drum tipping and tapping away
To the agile pipe that wriggles about like an eel.
Remember the group who sang in the café that day?
And the village fête on Sunday where we saw
The circle of life complete, saw the day
Turn from morning to night, from light to grey,
And the people counterwise from grave to gay,
From church to dance and then from dance to play.
Sunday morning, seven by the clock,
And the village silent except for the cock
Ricochetting far away: and over the roof
Are the dark Pyrenees, overweening and aloof
As ever. A boy comes into the square
And a pigeon rises and flashes the rosy air.
Never was morning so clear. And one by one
A rope of bees bubbles up into the sun.
A bell is calling the people to early Mass,
The doors open, I watch the church-goers pass
To where within the ancient womb
A blaze of incense and a bloom
Of candles ring the bridegroom-priest
Who bodies forth the Mystery
That has been all men's history:
Two thousand years behind him say
This is as it was in our day.
O how the grounded women sing
To galleried men all answering
As heaven answers earth.
Voice marries voice as if by choice;
And so the ancient circle's closed, the service done. See, there,
The man with the basket of plants outside the church,
Selling them to the farmers. But they leave him in the lurch;
They are eager to follow the band across the churchyard green
To the yellow Presbytery house, shaded by chestnuts and limes
And dappled by light, where numberless times
They have come about birth and death. But today they are free

To celebrate in a dance the curé's jubilee.
And now the red-sashed dancers, looking so cool and so clean,
Form themselves into a figure. The drummer wipes
His brow and begins to tap, and a young priest pipes.
And the curé comes out on the steps and smiles to see them so
    keen.
Yes. This morning the world went into the church.
Now the church comes into the world. So,
In life we oppose and appease each other.
And under the gentle trees the crowd gathers thicker and faster,
And a red setter dog looks everywhere for the curé, his master.
Now bright before our glance
Comes forth each white-clad mummer
To figure forth in a dance
The rise and fall of summer,
Needle-pipe and thimble-drum
Leading the way to kingdom-come.
Still oozes the old wound
The summer Prince is slain,
His blood's the poppy seed
That will rise up again
To fill the winter fields with newly-springing grain.
Afternoon, late afternoon, and the sun still hot,
As we cross the square. And all the houses have
A hat of plane-tree leaves pulled over their eyes
Against the light. But what a buzz and a fuzz
Of people are gathered to watch the *pelota*.
We can hear the *pock* of the ball against the great curved wall
Behind the church. And now we can see the players
With the basket-claws on their hands, scooping
And pawing the ball. A priest is swooping
Among them in magpie flight. He plays
In his long black robe; the others in white,
Sweeping like swallows across the court in the evening light.
Tiers on tiers of people are 'oh-ing!' and 'ah-ing!',
Watching and greeting with cries the well-placed shot.
How they mouth-in each move and stop of the ball!

And the cobbler is singing the score. The people cheer
The winning ball, and the band blares out 'all clear'.
And now the bubbling crowd boils over on to the court
To dance the evening through, until their throats are dry,
Dancing to the pipe and the little titupping drum.
And in the dusky cafés the lads and girls may be talking,
But as soon as the little drum blinks, all the talk goes blank;
A curly catching tune, and their trigger-feet are off
In a flash from the shadowy gloom,
Lads with billowing shirts, and girls with willowy skirts
Slanting along the street, linking hands as they go
In a fine kite-tail procession; or twirling toe to toe,
Weaving a wicker-work figure round all who won't give room.
And the listening moon comes up and looks down on the dizzy
    scene,
On the dancers flitting like moths round the group at the café
    table
Where two old dignified men are battling over a bottle
Twisting in wordy wedlock like eels all ready to throttle.
Outlay and intake of breath, rise and fall
Of a season, ins and outs of a dance.
Happy people. No greed for tomorrow
Greys your face like frost. O
May all your valleys be fat
With wine, and full be every vat.

THE JOURNEY OF THE MAGI

Behold there came wise men from the east, saying, Where is he, for we have seen his star?

It was a dark January night, cold and snowing
When the Three Kings started out
On their annual journey: and what on earth
They were doing—and such a time to be going!
And, honestly, what it was all about
Not one of them knew. But they wanted a birth,
A new lift, as we all do. Was the journey wise?—
Yes, or No? Well, that was anybody's guess
As it still is: a risk. A different address
May only land you in a different kind of a mess.
Put it no higher than that. But still, there was the Star
Throbbing in front like a bell, bobbing them on from afar,
Regardless of hail, rain, or snow, or glitter or glar.
The Three Kings marched away into the west,
To one dark enterprise they were addressed.
There was nowhere they would not go, feast or fast,
Slum or salon, bethel or brothel, if only at last
And at least they could come to the truth and be blessed.
Perhaps in some far corner of the world
An answer lay, a sleeping past was curled.
February now, the driving swathes of rain
Swaddle the hills that edge the Atlantic main,
And wave on wave like superimposing hands
Slip and withdraw on Europe's farthest strands.
Through the wet night the Three Kings rode away,
It mattered not who called on them to stay;
It matters not who dances or who sings
They must away to find the King of Kings.
To welcome gravity, and to forego fun
Is still their fate who seek the heavenly One
And choose the Star.

And now the month is March,
Bloodbursty buds are pink upon the larch.

One thing about journeys which is rather good
—Things never happen how and where they should.
God, for example, as the Three Kings found,
Is seldom above-board, but underground;
And on the other hand, the Devil
Is to be met on almost every level,
High place and holy day. The guide-book's Star
Has small relation to things as they are.
Still, one lives and learns that saints, if fat,
Are none the earthier or the worse for that;
God can be sought for in a golden rain
Of levity and fireworks; piety's not pain.
The guns go off, the rockets fly
Over the Kings now riding by.
In passing, one may duly note
That reverence need not choke the throat
Or dull the cheek.
It's only those
Who hug the sober truth, the gloomy ones,
Who always fear to let off their guns.
Truth's never sober, but, like a wayward gipsy
She wears the loudest colours, shouts, and goes half-tipsy.
Now up, now down, now gay, now melancholy,
Now drawn to hope and now pursued by folly,
The Three Kings marched zigzag, a star their brolly.
Caspar got blind one night, Melchior met a lady,
Balthazar was involved in something shady;
Strange that, in lands, and countries quite unknown,
We find, not others' strangeness, but our own;
That is one use of journeys; if one delves,
Differently, one's sure to find one's selves.
O in what wilderness of one another
We wander looking for ourselves! What bother
We go through, what cold, what heat
To find the answer up our own back street.
Meanwhile this gipsy life the Three Kings led, as unconfined
As the May bloom that blithely takes the wind.

A man comes up to the Three Kings and cries
'I'm an insurance agent; I advise—
In case you're tempted, sirs, to trust your eyes—
Take out a policy, against surprise.
Seeing's believing; journeys are dangerous things;
Belief can lay its icy hand on Kings.
For a small premium we will give relief
In case of sickness, second sight, belief;
But if at sixty-five you're still quite blind,
You'll get a bonus; our company's that kind.
Just answer these few questions:—Have you had
Father or Mother who was ill or mad
Or bad enough to see things as they are?
Did any of your family see a star?
Barring that——' With that they pushed the man away;
Live dangerously, see all, and come what may,
Was their belief.
The Three Kings hitched their wagon to the Star
And gave the Star its head. Now near, now far,
Now in, now out, now to and fro it led;
Never straight. Journeys are always curly,
Like comets or like hairpins they are meant
To crown or to lead up to some event.
Herod did all he could do to prevent
Their coming. This journey had its hazards.
He broke the poles, and he cut the wires,
He stole their pump and deflated their tyres,
And he turned their messengers into liars;
But in vain.
He muffled the knocker, disconnected the bell,
Turned up his radio till it howled like hell,
Changed his name and address as well;
But in vain.

After October with its fiery leaf
Came grey November, frozen, as in grief;
Dumpy with impotence King Herod sat,

Not even bothering to take off his hat,
When in came the Three Kings, as if by chance,
And Herod rose and made great song and dance
About them. Black Caspar said to Balthazar
'He's a good sort, Herod; there's no colour-bar
With him.' 'May be', said Melchior, 'but why
Does he keep staring up into the sky?
And why's he quizzing us about the Star?'
'O just some complex', Caspar said, 'to do with power:
Rank has its obligations, and in fact
The first is to preserve itself intact.'
—So they argued on, intent;
Till suddenly, above the Palace towers
They saw their guiding star turn red, like Mars,
And knew that it was angry. Bloody wars
It threatened. And at once they went
Without good-byes.

December now; the Three Kings stood
Benighted in the deepest wood,
The wits-end of their hardihood.
No longer kings, but helpless now
They threw away their golden bough;
They stamped upon their golden crowns
And damned the country, damned the towns.
They'd lost the Star, their only link
And anchor-light. O not a blink
No hope, no help in earth or sky!
—They gave a last despairing cry.
Then suddenly all raised a shout
For overhead the Star flared out
Just like a fan: and there they saw
In the last ditch, on the last straw,
In front of them a heavenly child.
See! it looked up at them and smiled.
It was the child within themselves
For which they'd sought, for which Age delves

—Now Age and Innocence can meet,
Now, now the circle is complete,
The journey's done. Lord, Lord, how sweet!

SONG FOR WAR

Put away the flutes
Into their careful clefts,
And cut the violins that like ivy climb
Flat to their very roots;
All that a subtler time
Allowed us we must now commute
To commoner modes; for here come
The hieratic trumpet and demotic drum.
Fall in and follow, let the beat
Hyphenate your halved feet,
Feel its imbricating rhythm
Obliterating every schism
And split through which you might espy
The idiosyncratic I;
Let the assumptive trumpets pace
And pattern out the sounding space
Into stillnesses that numb
By iteration and by sum,
Till the walls of will fall down
Round the seven-times-circled town
Of your mind, and not a jot
Is left of fore or after thought.
O slowly go and closely follow
Toe to heel and hill to hollow,
All the ditto feet that lead
You onward in a millipede
To the battle where, as one,
A hundred thousand tip and run.

But when the burning sun again
Behind the hill
Slides down and leaves the separate slain
Frosted and still,
Then over the rued fields that drum and trumpet fled
Slow musics rise like mists and wreathe their requiem
Round the bruised reeds, and coldly mounts the moon
Of thought, and rules among the quorum of the dead.

SONG FOR PEACE

See, the ruthless victor comes
With tooth of trumpet, claw of drums,
Have ready on his route
A fanfare of strumpets and a salute
of fifty bums;
This, this will be his randy-vous
With destiny; have handy, too,
The boostings of applause
To blow his fuses and effect a pause.
And you, you tuneless walls,
Open wide the windows of your huff
And hang out every hoarse hurrah,
Brighten your doorways, do your stuff,
And draw him from his coup d'état;
Bring out the dancing flute
And the frivolous fiddle,
Merry-go-round and inveigle
Him into the middle,
Until his sidelong glances scrape
Across the feminine violin-shape,
And his obedient battalions
Caper on curtseying feet like stallions.
Yet if this fails, fails to move
Him from his humdrummed groove,
And if the hammered round
Of order and routine
Allows no new, no extraordinary sound
To dent, to enter or to intervene;
If in the fixed receipt
Of war's auricular beat
He marches on unvarying and complete,
Then some disharmony we must devise
Him to divide against himself and civilize:
Then let the still small voice
Connive, contrive
To enter a caveat against
Each move by which he would arrive:

Veto no destination, but instead
Insert a doubt into his very tread;
See that his single track of feeling frays
Into two sudden, different, equal ways;
Between his 'I will' and 'I ought'
Cause him to halt and stand in thought;
Force him to pick and predicate
Each walking step and waking state;
Till his one-way-street of going
Vacillates into to-and-froing,
And his flowing roundabout
Of feeling flounders into doubt
And angular analysis
Of self and its paralysis.

At last, at last his listless hand lets fall
The pulseless drum,
And the uncertain trumpet asks
The way to kingdom-come,
And Peace comes forward now, him to inurn.
Ring bells, and bawl hooray,
Empty is war's highway,
And men to subtler routes and set pursuits return.
And yet,
As quavering rings of sound
Surround the clanged gong,
Wrinkling on long after and far out,
In mind we may prolong
Beyond the body's bound
The wavering flounces of that martial shout
That once called all men up and coiled them round
With rhythm that now is fallen utterly into rout.

NATIVITY

His holly hair, his berry eyes are here,
And his chrysanthemum wound,
This Christmas day; by symbols once again
The Mystery's importuned.

Hisses the singing kettle of his blood
Out of his sanguine side,
Poked by the sibling spear it ebbs and flows
In a hub-bubble tide

That dyes the silent room. The gay young god,
Dog in the manger now,
Growls in the hearth, and bares old teeth against
The Ass in us, the Cow.

There are the portly bottle-loins, and there
The wine-marks of his birth
Upon the straw, the biscuit-brittle straw
Broken by Mary's girth.

And here, most meek, most eager and most hushed,
The angelic agents hover,
A great prudential company, all come
To offer him life-cover.

Comes sentiment with frozen tears lent
By memory, melting sweet,
Her hothead cries boil over and congeal
Again at her cold feet.

And Grief, deep in her crushed and tinfoil wrap,
Brokenly glares today
Among the ashes and the cruel butt-
Ends of this Christmas play.

And there's the tapering tree of his descent,
Hitched to a kingly star,
Earth is its horizontal, heaven and hell
Its upright centre-spar.

The very tree of life, so base, so wide,
And with such longing fraught,
Up the step-ladder of our looks it spires
Into a point of thought.

In the stark winter of our tinselled pride
Its frozen growth now stands
Waiting the fiery gift, the melting dew
Spangled from heavenly hands.

Ah look! the bush is candleabraed now
With yellow and with blue,
Types of the spirit, sweet and bitter both,
Opposed but wholly true.

Outside, like rootless souls the silent trees
Sail past on trays of mist;
The miser-icicle on the pane still marks
The place that Judas kissed.

His thistle breath still lingers in the air,
Spiky with eagerness,
It hovers on the garden, and the grass
Whitens at his caress.

Robin with rusty bib no longer can
Pull out the worm-like nail,
Dumpy with impotence it droops and humps
Upon the wooden rail.

And hark! the Herod-angels sing tonight!
Over the Magi's tents
Their heartless song drones on through grumbling glooms
And weeping continents.

High on his farthing floor the airman moons
Above the mourning town
Of Bethlehem; it is his fiddling root
And he the flower and crown.

O Caspar, Melchior, and Balthazar,
Come from your caravan
And tell me where you go, and what new star
You saw in Teheran:

And what new man now hurries to be born
Out of our addled earth,
And O what silly corner of ourselves
Will see the mangy birth.

Strike, strike the gong of our song till souls take fire,
Clap hands and bellow,
Dance, dance, leap higher and longer, and hug
Each with its fellow.

Lord, in this wintry interval we send
Our indolent regards
And grey regrets. Make fluent all the pens
Of all the frozen bards.

Lay the live coal upon their lips that they
May leap uproariously
Out of their huff of words, and let the thorns
Crackle with prophecy.

Resume, and reimburse the silent wood,
Elaborate its saps,
Bid the bare trees blurt into bloom, and fill
With leaf the hungry gaps,
And in its head set the heart's singing birds.

NEITHER HERE NOR THERE

In that land all is, and nothing's ought;
No owners or notices, only birds;
No walls anywhere, only lean wire of words
Worming brokenly out from eaten thought;
No oats growing, only ankle-lace grass
Easing and not resenting the feet that pass;
No enormous beasts, only names of them;
No bones made, bans laid, or boons expected,
No contracts, entails, hereditaments,
Anything at all that might tie or hem.

In that land all's lackadaisical;
No lakes of coddled spawn, and no locked ponds
Of settled purpose, no netted fishes;
But only inkling streams and running fronds
Fritillaried with dreams, weedy with wishes;
Nor arrogant talk is heard, haggling phrase,
But undertones, and hesitance, and haze;
On clear days mountains of meaning are seen
Humped high on the horizon; no one goes
To con their meaning, no one cares or knows.

In that land all's flat, indifferent; there
Is neither springing house or hanging tent,
No aims are entertained, and nothing is meant,
For there are no ends and no trends, no roads,
Only follow your nose to anywhere.
No one is born there, no one stays or dies,
For it is a timeless land, it lies
Between the act and the attrition, it
Marks off bound from rebound, make from break, tit
From tat, also today from tomorrow.
No Cause there comes to term, but each departs
Elsewhere to whelp its deeds, expel its darts;
There are no homecomings, of course, no good-byes
In that land, neither yearning nor scorning,
Though at night there is the smell of morning.

THE TOWER

Pile upon pile of thought he drove
Into the sobbing bog below,
While others on the shaking raft
Of laughter travelled to and fro;
Light after light of love sailed by
His single and unseeing eye.

Coldly he willed and boldly strove
To build the lean and winding stair,
While, wide and high, the idle drove
Swung on hyperboles of air;
In hoops of happiness they curled
Bat-like about his darkening world.

Whose was the hand that laid the pyre?
What was the foot that fled the stair?
Look how the jarring tongues of fire
Roll out and glory-hole the air.
From the charred arches of his brain
The golden girders fall like rain
Upon the unforgiving plain.

SPRING

From my wind-blown book I look
Up and see the lazy rook
Rise and twist away,
And from every airy eave
The arrowy swallows wildly leave
And swoop as if in play.

Dark the daw with claw-wing sail
Swings at anchor in the gale,
And in the running grass
Daffodils nod and intervene
Like sud-flecks on a sea of green
Dissolving as they pass.

Mouldy and old the bouldered walls
Wake in the sun and warm their polls
And wag aubretia beards,
The snail-gaze of senility
Silvers each front, and backward they
Break wind and dree their weirds.

Bosoms of bloom that sob like moss
Beneath each jumpy breath, emboss
The bony orchard's breast;
And look, the leggy lilac canes
Are varicosed with ivy veins
Of envy coalesced.

There the hare, bound after bound,
Concertinas all the ground
As far as eye can spy it,
Like a fountain's dying spray
It falls in little frills away
Into a twitching quiet.

Still down the slow opposing slope
The intent ploughman draws his rope
Of parsimony fine,
Nor sees bold Icarus in his haste
Expend his spirit in a waste
Of aerobatic wine.

Icarus from his heady plane
Into depths of spinning brain
Bales out like a ball,
Pulls the ripcord, splits the sack
And lets the spilled silk splutter back
And speculative fall.

And hark, the lark sarcastic sings
To Icarus without his wings
Dawdling down the sky,
Indolent aeons have gone to make
Its gimlet bill, its song-gill's shake,
Its all-containing cry.

AUTUMN DAY

Going out, those bold days,
O what a gallery-roar of trees and gale-wash
Of leaves abashed me, what a shudder and shore
Of bladdery shadows dashed on windows ablaze,
What hedge-shingle seething, what vast lime-splashes
Of light clouting the land. Never had I seen
Such a running-over of clover, such tissue sheets
Of cloud poled asunder by sun, such plunges
And thunder-load of fun. Trees, grasses, wings—all
On a hone of wind sluiced and sleeked one way,
Smooth and close as the pile of a pony's coat,
But, in a moment, smoke-slewed, glared, squinted back
And up like sticking bones shockingly unkinned.
How my heart, like all these, was silk and thistle
By turns, how it fitted and followed the stiff lifts
And easy falls of them, or, like that bird above me,
No longer crushing against cushions of air,
Hung in happy apathy, waiting for wind-rifts.
Who could not dance on, and be dandled by, such a day
Of loud expansion? when everyflash and shout
Took the hook of the mind and reeled out the eye's line
Into whips and whirl-spools of light, when every ash-shoot shone
Like a weal and was gone in the gloom of the wind's lash.
Who could not feel it? the uplift and total subtraction
Of breath as, now bellying, now in abeyance,
The gust poured up from the camp's throat below, bringing
Garbled reports of guns and bugle-notes.
But, gullible, then drank them back again.
And I, dryly shuffling through the scurf of leaves
Fleeing like scuffled toast, was host to all these things;
In me were the spoon-swoops of wind, in me too
The rooks dying and settling like tea-leaves over the trees;
And, rumbling on rims of rhyme, mine were the haycarts home-
    creeping
Leaving the rough hedge-cheeks long-strawed and streaked with
    their weeping.

HOME THOUGHTS FROM ABROAD

Hearing, this June day, the thin thunder
Of far-off invective and old denunciation
Lambasting and lambegging the homeland,
I think of that brave man Paisley, eyeless
In Gaza, with a daisy-chain of millstones
Round his neck; groping, like blind Samson,
For the soapy pillars and greased poles of lightning
To pull them down in rains and borborygmic roars
Of rhetoric. (There but for the grace of God
Goes God.) I like his people and I like his guts
But I dislike his gods who always end
In gun-play. Some day, of course, he'll be one
With the old giants of Ireland—such as
Denis of the Drought, or Iron-Buttocks—
Who had at last to be reduced to size,
Quietly shrunken into 'wee people'
And put out to grass on the hills for good,
Minimized like cars or skirts or mums;
Photostatted to fit a literate age
And filed safely away on the dark shelves
Of memory; preserved in ink, oak-gall,
Alcohol, aspic, piety, wit. A pity,
Perhaps, if it is drama one wants. But,
Look at it this way: in this day and age
We can't really have giants lumbering
All over the place, cluttering it up,
With hair like ropes, flutes like telegraph poles,
And feet like tramcars, intent only on dogging
The fled horse of history and the Boyne.
So today across the Irish Sea I wave
And wish him well from the bottom of my heart
Where truth lies bleeding, its ear-drums burst
By the blatter of his hand-me-down talk.
In fond memory of his last stand
I dedicate this contraceptive pill
Of poetry to his unborn followers,
And I place
This bunch of beget-me-nots on his grave.

THOUGHTS IN A DRY SEASON

Rhodesia, Vietnam, the lot, how it all
Ekes out endlessly. It is an ill blow, they say,
That winds nobody good and proper;
At least my father said so, though I
Was never any good at blows, and bad
At carrying the can for the executioner:
Can, parental rod, schoolmaster's cane, it was all
The same; usually I dropped it, or failed
To come back with it when sent,
Until they had forgotten why I went
Or came. 'Slow-coach!' my mother said, 'You would be
A good one to send for sorrow.'
I never wanted to become a man
Of the world, and now that I have come
Late and loathfully to years of wisdom
And discretion I want only
To become the world of man who travels
Slowly with the stick, cosh, baton, gas-canister
They sent him for, still hoping
That he won't get back too quick,
In time to cope or cop it properly.
Idiot! Why should I trust these times or look
For rhyme or reason in them, since it's clear
That nothing's changed,
That whips won't flog themselves to death
Or nooses choke for want of breath
This year.

SCAPEGOAT

God broke into my house last night
With his flying-squad, narks, batmen, bully-boys,
Proctors, bailiffs, aiders and abettors—
Call them what you will—hard-mouthed, bowler-hatted.
Hearing a lack of noise I had gone downstairs
To let the dog out.
The tall figure with his obedient shadows
Pushed past me into the light and turned
With the accusing document; all my fears.
It seemed I had for years out of mind
Owed him a sum of money and had paid
Nothing. 'Lord,' I said reluctantly, looking
Into his implacably-forgiving face,
'I would have called it a lie, but if you
Say so, it must be so.'
I do not know—
It being a dream of sorts—I do not know
If it were His son or my son
The doomsmen laid upon the floor then,
The knife to his throat.
I saw no more. But the dog of the house
Fled howling through the open door.

LAMENT FOR AN EDUCATED
HOLE IN THE ROAD

Some creep stole a hole last night
Out of our L. A. Freeway, and left
Only a blinking collar of lights
Barking at us in the dark.
A jumbo-hole too;
The sheer barebacked effrontery of it!
Any punk who'd do a thing like that
Deserves to have a daisy-chain of milestones
Tied round his neck and drowned in the hole he stole:
Education in depth, as Boss Rafferty
Calls it. Oh I know,
A hole is nothing, you say; but nix on that!
There's nothing like an educated hole
To slow the swine down and put a drop
On progress. As simple as that. Academically,
A hitch in time saves nine, nor could clerk care less.
A hole is a full stop, a think tank,
A night-stick for eggheads, highbrows, cleaver-pushers,
Sour grapepickers, protestors, and all damn fools
Who want bread on their jam.
There's no knowing what a hole's about;
That is the beauty of it.
A hole is silence, is topless. A hole is a shout
Turned inside out to warn every lout,
Skunk, dove, screwball, crackpot who spouts
Peace, ethnic needs, civil rights, goodwill,
Welfare, minicare, and what-have-you,
To stow it: no use having a good word to say
If you've gotten a bad breath. Look at it
In the round, just. A hole is an O, like in
Order, Cop, property-lot, politics,
Oil, development, motivation, goal.
It is the mouthpiece of democracy.
It is the still small voice that is inside
Every redwood asking to be cut down;
It is the White House that is inside

Every log-cabin, crying to be let out;
It is the pinprick in the contraceptive
Of the explosive American dream.
It is maximum opportunity.
It is open to all. It is for free.
It is truly ecumenical. In fact
A hole is everything you dig that isn't
Yet. Put it on stilts you get a heaven
Los Angelically speaking, or
A governor, Sacramentotal.

No, Mister Rafferty, that hole that was stole
On you last night couldn't have walked itself. Either
It was open-ended, in which case
It was a drop-out, or—What's that?
The hole was elastic? It's still
There? Elephant? What Elephant? Oh sure, sure,
I remember now. It there too? Man,
That's what comes of californicating
With McCarthy. Elephantiasis
All round. Holes are total.

THE FOUNTAIN
IN THE PUBLIC SQUARE

                        Once more it is a day
For ever. In the empty square
Morning puts up a fountain for
Election to the light.
I am always surprised by fountains,
By their bland assumption that air is still
Deserving of them, that it will roundly
Uphold them like ropes. To have such high hopes
Of heaven argues pin-upness of sorts,
A hang-god belief in hooks or *hagios*. Yet
They are dryly let down. I have seen it done;
I have seen a whole huff of hair-fine individuals
Carried away scare-high on a waft of fun
To a rough drop, windjammed into one.
True water always wants away, wants
To run, is worldly wide. It knows
The nerve of the land as smoke knows
The swerve of air, is seldom taken in
By lies of leniency.
Of course a river has its reveries;
It may pretend to boggle at a drop,
May pool its looks and stop, but not for long.
Even canals, however sunk in thought,
Have somewhere outlet. But fountains, no!
Fountains are for show, and are not
Above repeating themselves. They go
To endless roundabouts to stand and gloat,
Fixed as a cliché in the stony throat
Of some oracular square.

                        You'd swear they were
Pleased with the business of just being there.
Fountains, like conifers (that sneeze of needles
With noses in the air) are sticklers for
Formality. Summit and symmetry
Are what they want. Give them a dotted line

To toe they do it on their heads
And never turn a hair. They were not meant
To tint the wind with wonder or with wildness.
Their wits were never wandering ones like water.
Their sin is sameness and their stint is stone.
I'd rather have the fickle run of things
Like rivers any day. Stone is static,
Is pat. Water alone is love, all else
Is law and fixity. Still,
For us whose sin is to have no centre,
Who have twelve every ways for one thing,
This pensive fountain in the empty square
Is our best summing-up, a sign
Of godlike self-possession and belonging
That we raise against these scattering days
Of endless means and meaningless ends.
In a stone bowl
Life stays.
Clamatory as a gong
With its collateral rings of calm
Each congregated fountain roundly says
'I am.' That is the heart of the matter.
All else is water.

SPANISH DANCER

A pause, and then the glass hands
Broke into applause.
A figure had come upon the stage:
A most dumb image
Of studied doom
And fixed Promethean gloom
Stood there in a rage
Of grief, hands choked.

What wind wrested his roots
As he stood there? What air
Wrung his wrist to that exquisite reach
And inch-stint of longing?
Never have I seen such a curling grief
Of caterpillaring fingers clinging
To an eaten end-leaf's quivering vein
No, not since my knees (Antonio)
Were no bigger than beads strung on a thread of blood
Have I known such a shivering foot and goat's toe
Of sheer alacrity.
Were you born between two flints to scintillate so?
At your incomparable feet, they tell me,
The nervous lightnings romped and loitered
Humbly, and when you stumbled
The thunder learned its accomplished clumsiness.

WINTER'S COLD

May, and the wall was warm again. For miles
The welcoming air was lighted with smiles
Of homecoming hawthorn. Beat any bush
And a dust of birds flew out: lift a leaf,
There was laughter under. It was a day
For overtones and reveries of thunder.
Everyone walked in a haze, everything
Had a glory of stillness about it: hills
Had their hold-back of story. What shadow
Chilled our talk then? What high word screamed and was gone
Between us? Somewhere in air we heard it,
A stinging thong and rising weal of sound
Like a whoop and whip-round of bees swinging
Above the trees. She shivered, as if to say
'All the hives of our heart have swarmed today.'
Well, we hurriedly tried all sorts of things,
Drenched them in tears of protestation,
Ran everywhere, rooted out old buckets
Of goodwill, rattled odd tin-cans of kinship,
Looked up, of course, the book of usages,
But it was all no good: we could retract
Nothing. Silently
We watched the singing skein of our hopes
Unreel and roll across country
In the calm weather. Has anyone heard
Of them since? Is it, in a sense, only
The winter's cold that holds us together, lonely?

REQUIEM FOR MICHAEL

Killed in an Essex road accident

If dumb stone
Can spare a spark of praise
For the blind ferrule of the stick that strikes it,
Why should we,
Who have the word for dumbness, not raise
Out of our inmost heart of stone
A striking phrase or two to mark
And mitigate our parting with this boy.

It is time
To articulate grief
And to name it. To name is to numb.
Relief is in the ritual. Therefore
Prepare the cheeks for pallor. Bring out now
The dark horses with their predicated paces
And dispassionate gloom. Summon the great words
From their habitual public play
And rehearsal rooms
To mouth him to his seldom tomb today.

A thinking bell,
Like a trifling failure of silence,
Spells aloud his eighteen proud years
Of weather-vane-glory.
All flesh is grass, intones the Preacher,
It is cut down, and withereth. Understatement of stone
Thinned to innuendo. Words, wind-worn to bone,
Reach us. A grief of fingers fidgets
In each glove. Around us, tip-toppled,
The leaden doves indicate love's dead-end.

Forgive us
This day our daily bread,
And remember our dead, Lord, especially this
Innumerable school-boy who
On Sunday morning cycled out of life

Before he knew it; head down
As if in a book. Screech of brakes
Like squeal of chalk on blackboard
Snapped the last word. The day broke
Its promise to him. His shadow fled.

Long-away
And far-ago, hungry
For learning, he left a Scottish croft
For these predestined fields.
The justified skies sang, and elected silence
Opened the book of his hands and read
The man-meanings. All the English signposts
Ran to meet him. And that young girl, his sister,
Who stands there so still,
Danced under the apple-tree he had planted on the hill.

Memory
Is what we forget with.
Today, this funeral day,
Chancing to pass her gate
I suddenly saw
That gay unthinking girl
Dancing there like water,
A flower stuck in her hair,
Dancing again like laughter.
Woodenly I stood
And watched her wicked step.
What could I do but stare
(Seeing in her no treason
But only body's reason)
Until she turned to look?

And I say—
True to form and to fern
The river runs forever,
Never once does the land

141

Ask it to what lengths
It is prepared to go.
Each step is a reason
For going farther.

FIELD DAY

The old farmer, nearing death, asked
To be carried outside and set down
Where he could see a certain field
'And then I will cry my heart out', he said.

It troubles me, thinking about that man;
What shape was the field of his crying
In Donegal?

I remember a small field in Down, a field
Within fields, shaped like a triangle.
I could have stood there and looked at it
All day long.

And I remember crossing the frontier between
France and Spain at a forbidden point, and seeing
A small triangular field in Spain,
And stopping

Or walking in Ireland down any rutted by-road
To where it hit the highway, there was always
At this turning-point and abutment
A still centre, a V-shape of grass
Untouched by cornering traffic,
Where country lads larked at night.

I think I know what the shape of the field was
That made the old man weep.

A LAST WORD

For Louis MacNeice d. September 1963

Only a green hill
And a man with a spade
Opening the old accounts-book of earth
And writing *paid*.

Under the highly improbable sky,
Needlessly blue,
He piles the cold clay. It is all,
You might say, so dead true

To life, the meek clay turning the other cheek
To the clap of the spade
Waits to inherit the earth of the man
Whom it has made.

But he made it
That made him,
He put the word on it that gave
Life and limb.
Now to speak of an end
Is to begin.

APPENDIX

EPILOGUE

to 'The Character of Ireland'[1]

Here I come, always in at the tail-end.
A good man for a funeral or a wake;
Patient in graveyards, used to thinking long
And walking short, remembering what
My careful father told me—'If ever, son,
You have to go anywhere and have to
Run, never go! It's unlucky.' 'Slow-coach!'
My mother used to call me. 'You,' she said,
'Would be a good one to send for sorrow.'
I had a tongue in both my parents' cheeks,
Could take the word out of two different mouths,
But chose my father's slower way of talk
That had the native tint of wonder in it
To soften it; though my mother tongue,
Scots, raucous, quick, followed it hard
With hints of glottal stops.
I am Ulster, my people an abrupt people
Who like the spiky consonants in speech
And think the soft ones cissy; who dig
The *k* and *t* in orchestra, detect sin
In sinfonia, get a kick out of
Tin cans, fricatives, fornication, staccato talk,
Anything that gives or takes attack,
Like Micks, Tagues, tinkers' gets, Vatican.
An angular people, brusque and Protestant,
For whom the word is still a fighting word,
Who bristle into reticence at the sound
Of the round gift of the gab in Southern mouths.
Mine were not born with silver spoons in gob,
Nor would they thank you for the gift of tongues;
The dry riposte, the bitter repartee's
The Northman's bite and portion, his deep sup
Is silence; though, still within his shell,
He holds the old sea-roar and surge

[1] See p. xi. This text of the 'Epilogue' is a conflation of WRR's version of 28 May 1963 and a later two-page manuscript draft of the first 59 lines.

147

Of rhetoric and Holy Writ.
Three hundred years ago our foundling fathers
With farthing fists and thistles in their eyes
Were planted on this foreshore,
Bibles for bibs and bloody pikes for rattles
And tombs for keeps. There was not time
To wade through wedding to a birth.
Calvin and culverin sang the cradle-song
And Cromwell made the bed.
Put to a frugal breast of swollen hopes
They did their levelling best and left it flat
As water. Winding-sheet and swaddling-band
Were one. Needle-flute and thimble-drum
Stitched the way to kingdom-come, to Derry,
Aughrim, Enniskillen, and the Boyne:
Rat-a-ta-ta, rat-a-ta-ta, rat-a-ta-ta,
Humdrummery of history.
And I, born to the purple passage,
Was heir to all that Adamnation
And hand-me-down of doom, the late comer
To the worn-out womb.
The apple blushed for me below Bellevue,
Lagan was my Jordan, Connswater
My washpot, and over Belfast
I cast out my shoe.

(I describe childhood in Belfast. The 'Troubles'. The Enemy. The getting to know the Enemy, and liking him, which is 'growing-up'. Every à deux is an à quatre. The Crossing of the Border for the first time.)

To Dublin then I came, burning, burning, burning.
By the waters of Liffey I sat down and wept.
I hanged my harp upon a Guinness tree
And wept—being parsimonious—with one eye
At a time; once for life and once for joy,
First a girl and then a boy:
After life's fitful fever we weep well.

(What do I weep for? I weep for Wapping Pier, where, for two years, I lived and loved—'Sweet Thames run softly till I end my song'— and for the Unborn, *for the endless flottilas of F.L.S. that floated inflatedly, endlessly, all day down-river there—The Thames. I compare it with The Liffey—clearly uncontracepted—and I weep for the* Born, *for the Emigrants, for the writing on the North Wall, for the Country that couldn't contain its own, for Swift, Burke, Wilde, Shaw, Yeats, Joyce—all of whom left it at the age of 21,— 'centre of paralysis'—etc; 'The Great Hunger', two 'megadeaths': The 'Navigators'.*

I start on my favourite theme, the characteristics of Irishmen, and illustrate it:—Yeats talking about Synge; Synge talking about Yeats; O'Connell about himself; Fox about Burke; Lord Derwent about Joyce (at his funeral); Joyce about the church; Everybody about everybody. But for the first time I realise I have to find a way of putting this in some sort of verse or rhythmic prose.)

The Irish bell was tongueless once. Now all
Our bells have tongues in cheek.

(I think you'll understand I'm troubled now, and working. I don't know how the thing will end. Probably with an invocation—)

Pray for me, publicans of Belfast, Dublin Galway, Bunraw,
Pray for me presbyters and priests and piddlers
of Armagh, Augher, Glogher, Five-Mile-Town,
Pray for me, Shopkeepers, gombeen men of Abbeyfeale,
Rosegreen, How-are-you,
And may God save Ireland from her heroes
For what we need is not heroism,
But normal courage.